PLAYS FROM VAULT 3

TUMULUS
Christopher Adams

GLITTER PUNCH
Lucy Burke

BURKAS AND BACON BUTTIES
Shamia Chalabi & Sarah Henley

WIND BIT BITTER, BIT BIT BIT HER
Sami Ibrahim

THE STRONGBOX
Stephanie Jacob

Also Available from Nick Hern Books

PLAYS FROM VAULT

EGGS
Florence Keith-Roach

MR INCREDIBLE
Camilla Whitehill

PRIMADONNA
Rosie Kellett

CORNERMEN
Oli Forsyth

RUN
Stephen Laughton

PLAYS FROM VAULT 2

TESTAMENT
Tristan Bernays

SAVE + QUIT
Sophia Leuner

WRETCH
Rebecca Walker

THIS MUST BE THE PLACE
Brad Birch & Kenneth Emson

MAISIE SAYS SHE LOVES ME
Jimmy Osborne

PLAYS FROM VAULT 3

TUMULUS
Christopher Adams

GLITTER PUNCH
Lucy Burke

BURKAS AND BACON BUTTIES
Shamia Chalabi & Sarah Henley

WIND BIT BITTER, BIT BIT BIT HER
Sami Ibrahim

THE STRONGBOX
Stephanie Jacob

NICK HERN BOOKS

London
www.nickhernbooks.co.uk

A Nick Hern Book

Plays from VAULT 3 first published in Great Britain in 2018 as a paperback original by Nick Hern Books Limited, The Glasshouse, 49a Goldhawk Road, London W12 8QP, in association with VAULT Festival

Tumulus copyright © 2018 Christopher Adams
Glitter Punch copyright © 2018 Lucy Burke
Burkas and Bacon Butties copyright © 2018 Shamia Chalabi, Sarah Henley
Wind Bit Bitter, Bit Bit Bit Her copyright © 2018 Sami Ibrahim
The Strongbox copyright © 2018 Stephanie Jacob

The authors have asserted their moral rights

Cover image by Crucible Creative

Designed and typeset by Nick Hern Books, London
Printed and bound in Great Britain by Mimeo Ltd, Huntingdon, Cambridgeshire PE29 6XX

A CIP catalogue record for this book is available from the British Library

ISBN 978 1 84842 737 2

Woodland CARBON
www.woodlandcarbon.co.uk
NICK HERN BOOKS
Printed on Carbon Captured paper

Contents

Welcome (Back) to VAULT

We once dreamed about offering the chance for talented writers at VAULT to see their work published. (Enter Nick Hern Books, confident, bold, even foolhardy.) Three years on, and *Plays from VAULT* is becoming a festival staple. It's energising to know that there is interest in, and demand for, the VAULT alumni of 2018.

This year, these committed and passionate publishers have gone a step further, becoming the sole sponsors of the VAULT New Writers Award. Alongside writer Camilla Whitehill, and producer Rosalyn Newbery, eight brand-new playwrights are taking part in an eight-week writers' course at VAULT. It wouldn't have happened without Nick Hern Books and they deserve loud thanks for their belief in nurturing new talent.

VAULT 2018, the sixth festival, runs for eight weeks. We are joined by more venues than ever including the Waterloo East Theatre, the Network Theatre, and the Travelling Through Bookshop. There are already over 330 groups of artists featured in the programme at this year's festival.

If you're reading this, there's a good chance you're already curious, so forgive us if we co-opt you a little further. If you're good at being an audience member, come and see more than you planned to at VAULT. If you're good at being an artist, think about bringing something to VAULT 2019. If you're good at being a commissioner, you can go right ahead and commission these writers.

To the future!

Mat Burt, Andy George & Tim Wilson
VAULT Festival Directors

Biographies

CHRISTOPHER ADAMS

Christopher Adams is a British-American playwright. He has received short-play commissions from the Royal Court and Theatre503, and his plays *Lynchburg* (2013) and *Haunts* (2015) made the top-forty list for the Bruntwood Prize. His adaptation of *Antigone* recently toured nationally with Actors of Dionysus. He has been a member of the Royal Court Young Writers' Programme, Studio Writers' Group, Orange Tree Writers' Collective, the Arcola Writers' Group, and Playdate.

LUCY BURKE

Lucy is a Manchester-born writer living in London. She trained at Mountview Academy of Theatre Arts, graduating in 2015. Her play *Glitter Punch* has had critically acclaimed runs at the King's Head Theatre, London, and Assembly George Square Studios, Edinburgh Festival Fringe. It was also selected for the Pint-Size Plays new-writing initiative (Bunker Theatre, London), and was shortlisted for the Bolton Octagon Top Five Season.

Other writing credits include *WEIRD* (Arcola, SLAM Soaps); *Blackout* (Theatre N16, N16 Presents); *A Series of Unfortunate Breakups* (C Venues, Edinburgh Fringe Festival); *Funeral Parlour* (Royal Exchange Studio, Platform 1).

Lucy also heads up Some Riot Theatre Company, which she set up on graduating. Some Riot Theatre is an emerging company specialising in female-led new writing, and focusing on providing employment for graduate actors.

Lucy is a member of the Soho Theatre Young Writer's Lab '18. She likes to write plays set in and around the North of England, inspired by her northern heritage.

SHAMIA CHALABI

Shamia Chalabi graduated from the ArtsEd Acting course and is a London-based writer and actress working in theatre and TV.

This is Shamia's first full-length play, it is semi-autobiographical and based on some of her personal experiences growing up. Being brought up in London and Wigan she was exposed to a clash of cultures, this alongside her own mix of Egyptian/English heritage opened her eyes to the comedy that can be born out of the need to belong and keep everyone happy.

SARAH HENLEY

Sarah Henley originally trained in law and then as a performer at the London School of Musical Theatre. She was Writer's Assistant to Jeffrey Lane (Tony Award winner) on the West End production of *Women on the Verge of a Nervous Breakdown* and was listed on the BBC New Talent Hotlist in 2017. Her play for Delirium Theatre, *From Where I'm Standing* received five-star reviews and *The Stage*'s 'Must See' badge in Edinburgh. Writing credits include *Getting Out, Getting Away*, *After the Turn*, *Cinderella*, *From Where I'm Standing*, *Streets* (Offie nomination for Best New Musical and Most Promising Playwright), *Another Way* (Offie nomination for Best New Musical), *Muted* (Offie nomination for Best New Musical).

SAMI IBRAHIM

Sami Ibrahim is a young writer from London. His show *Iron Dome Fog Dome* was performed at The Yard during the latest First Drafts season. He has worked at the Almeida Theatre as a member of their Creative Board, developing and producing *From the Ground Up*, a piece of immersive theatre which went up to Edinburgh last summer. At the same time, he wrote and directed *Force of Trump*, a satire about Donald Trump becoming president. The show had runs at several theatres across London, including the Brockley Jack, where his short play, *Carnivore*, was also performed as part of the Write Now 7 Festival. He has taken part in The North Wall's Summer Residency Programme and is currently a member of Soho Theatre's Writers' Alumni Group.

STEPHANIE JACOB

Stephanie Jacob is a writer and actor.

Her first play, *Harry's Window*, about sibling rivalry among the over-eighties, had readings at the New Ambassadors, Soho Theatre and the National Theatre Studio, where Stephanie has subsequently been a Writer-on-Attachment.

The Quick, about restorative justice, was produced at the Tristan Bates Theatre, London, and was Time Out Critics' Choice for its run ('a tough and touching new play... fitting wit into the anguish... ever more tender' *Time Out*; 'clever and sharp, not easy to watch but very rewarding viewing' *A Younger Theatre*).

Her radio play, *A Night Visitor*, about a transformative pig (BBC Radio 4 Afternoon Drama), won the Writers' Guild Best Radio Drama Award.

Again, a new play about a family evolving after a divorce, will premiere at Trafalgar Studios in the West End in February 2018.

As an actor, Stephanie has worked at the National Theatre, RSC, in repertory, touring theatre and in the West End.

This book went to press before the end of rehearsals and so the texts may differ slightly from the plays as performed.

TUMULUS

Christopher Adams

For Tim, and Auntie Em

Tumulus was first performed at VAULT Festival, London, on 24 January 2018, with the following cast:

IAN HALLARD
TOM RHYS HARRIES
CIARÁN OWENS

Director	Matt Steinberg
Producer	Joanne L Williams
Designer	Alison Neighbour
Sound Designer	Nick Manning
Lighting Designer	Lucy Adams
Stage Manager	Megan Bly
Illustrator	Will Adams
Movement Director	Natasha Harrison
Filmmaker	Ciara O'Grady

This production acknowledges support received from Arts Council England.

4

Characters

Suggested doubling:

Male, thirties
ANTHONY

Male, early twenties	*Male, forties*
MATT	SIMON
VIJAY	CHRIS
SAM	OLLIE
CARL	MIKE
GEORGE	JOE
JONATHAN	NEWSPAPER
HENRY	COUNSELLOR
WILLIAM	PLACARD
JACK (THE YOUNGER)	GENE
CALLUM	JACK (THE ELDER)
OFFICER B	EDWARD
A, C, E, G, J	CHRISTOPHER
	FELIX
	MARTIN
	TEXT
	OWEN
	PERCY
	OFFICER A
	VOICEMAIL
	B, D, F, H, I

Setting

North London, the modern day.

Note on Text

Text in square brackets is unspoken.

ACT ONE

Scene One

ANTHONY
On a Saturday night in January
I arrive at a flat
In Willesden Green
There are six
Seven
Guys here already
They greet me like an old friend

    SIMON
    Hey

    MATT
    Hey

    CHRIS
    Hey man
    Good to see you

    VIJAY
    What's up?
    Haven't seen you in a while

    OLLIE
    How's you?

    SAM
    Heya

    MIKE
    Hey
    You're Roger right?

ANTHONY
Anthony
Actually

Like me they have been going for eighteen hours
One guy
(Simon?)
Has brought his pug

>SIMON
>Her name is Marigold
>Isn't she gorgeous?

ANTHONY
She's ghastly

Another
(Matt?)
Rushed from his shift at the Royal Free
His nursing scrubs are piled in a corner
He says to me

>MATT (*holding out a pair of shorts*)
>Here
>Put these on

ANTHONY
Thanks
But I have my own

The Uber from Kentish Town
Took about twenty minutes
Along the way I started to hear the sound

Sound.

This is generally my cue
That it's time for another hit

I find the kitchen
I am pleased to see Wandering Joe
He crops up at parties like these across North London
He brings a comforting air of middle management
The type of man who would feature
In a diarrhoea advertisement
An Excel spreadsheet is in front of him

I'm due

>JOE
>One hour?

ANTHONY
One hour exactly

Joe adds my name to his spreadsheet

> JOE
> I'm adding your name to my spreadsheet

ANTHONY
He notes the time

> JOE
> 1 32 a.m.

ANTHONY
He's precise

> JOE
> A good accountant should always be precise

ANTHONY
He sticks a syringe
Into a small bottle of clear liquid
He offers me a choice

> JOE
> Apple juice
> Or Lucozade?

ANTHONY
Apple
(I always have it with apple)
He drops the liquid in

> JOE
> One millilitre
> Two millilitres
> All done
> Don't want to kill you

ANTHONY
He tells me to chug it

> JOE
> Chug it

ANTHONY *drinks.*

He makes a face to indicate how awful it tastes.

ANTHONY
I wander back into the living room
The flat is clean
(Not like other flats I've been in)
But only because there is very little in it
The only books are
Two self-help works
And a biography of Thatcher
They aren't alphabetised

Some guys have their tops off
There are flecks of powder
Meow
M-cat
M
Scattered around
But no Tina
No pins
No one slamming into their veins
This is a classy party
Not like the party I will end up in
By hour forty

After a few moments
It starts
My limbs
(Previously solid and cumbersome)
Begin to loosen
I feel made of cartilage instead of bone
I realise I am attractive
Confident
And though Wandering Joe is the only person
Whose name I can accurately recall
Suddenly I feel I know
The intimate lives of every guy around me
We are like live wires plugged into the same circuit
And crucially
Crucially
The sound that began in the Uber

Sound.

Disappears

The sound fades.

I spot a guy in the corner

> CARL
> Want a bump?

ANTHONY *takes a bump*.

ANTHONY
Thanks

> CARL
> I'm Carl

ANTHONY
I'm Anthony

Carl is short but lithe
His ears are like teacups
He is young
Twenty-two at most
(I myself am not yet thirty-three)

Carl has a spot of fluff on his T-shirt

You have a spot of fluff on your T-shirt

> CARL
> Would you like to remove it?

ANTHONY
I am a librarian
I appreciate order

ANTHONY *removes the spot of fluff*.

> CARL
> Come sit on the sofa with me

CARL *takes* ANTHONY *by the hand*.

ANTHONY
I am about to follow Carl
When in the corner of my eye
I see someone
I do not expect to see
I am confused
The connection to every man in the room

Diminishes slightly
I consider that I might be hallucinating
Though that normally doesn't happen until hour seventy-two
I say

George?

He says

> GEORGE
> Yes?

ANTHONY
What are you doing here?

> GEORGE
> Will you give me a blowjob?

ANTHONY
This isn't that kind of party
(At least not yet)
Besides
Don't you think it would be difficult
Given the circumstances?

> GEORGE
> Oh you mean

ANTHONY
You're dead

> GEORGE
> Is that a problem?

ANTHONY
I must be hallucinating

I'm sorry
I'm just not sure it's possible
And even so

> GEORGE
> Even so what?

ANTHONY
Normally I would not insult someone
To their face

But the chems make you say
Exactly what you feel

I don't give blowjobs to men
Who are careless enough to die of an overdose
You give the rest of us a bad name

George's death was announced
In the Thursday edition of the *Ham and High*
(I am a subscriber)
George's body had been found
On the tumulus
The mound on the east side of the Heath
The headline read

> NEWSPAPER
> The body of George Carnick
> Twenty, of Dollis Hill
> Discovered by dog walker

ANTHONY
And a little later

> NEWSPAPER
> Police confirmed the cause of death
> Was an overdose of gamma-butyrolactone
> (GBL)

ANTHONY
We had met the usual way
The Yellow Monster

What's up?

> GEORGE
> Not much
> You?

ANTHONY
I like your necklace

> GEORGE
> My mum gave it to me
> To ward off evil

ANTHONY
Wanna come over and let me fuck you?

GEORGE
Sure

ANTHONY
The sex was functional
He was young
Not yet twenty-one
He assumed that youth
Could make up for technique
But I didn't care
I was high
Besides
I'm attracted to guys who face challenges in life
Like being left-handed
Or ginger
George was both

When we were done
He asked if he could stay

GEORGE
Can I stay?
Just for the night

ANTHONY
But I had learned that
Sleeping with another guy is dangerous
You might get used to him
Besides
George was not yet twenty-one
He was only useful for one thing

Sorry
There are guys you fuck
And guys you sleep with
And you're just a fuck

GEORGE
Oh

ANTHONY
I can see Carl growing bored
As he waits for me on the sofa

GEORGE
If you won't give me a blowjob then
I need to tell you something
My necklace is missing
The eye
To ward off evil

ANTHONY
A bit late for that
Don't you think?
Now if you'll excuse me

GEORGE
Please
I need it
To help me through to the other side
I think my killer has it

ANTHONY
What?

GEORGE
I didn't overdose

ANTHONY
The *Ham and High* said you did

GEORGE
I would never be that careless

ANTHONY
It was true
On our second hook-up
George produced a syringe and bottle
All his own

Apple or Lucozade?

GEORGE
Neither
I hate apples
And Lucozade gives me a rash
And makes me vomit

ANTHONY
Then who were you with
The night you were drugged?

> GEORGE
> I can't remember

ANTHONY
Carl is starting to talk to another guy
Who also appears to be not yet thirty-three
But somehow
Cooler
Hipper
Than I am
And wearing an ironic Transformers jumper
I want to rip it off him
And shove it down his throat
I have little choice but to say to George

I don't have time for this

> GEORGE
> We shared something

ANTHONY
You were just a fuck
Now leave me alone

> GEORGE
> We saw each other
> Fourteen times
> In the space of two months
> You said you were starting to have feelings

ANTHONY
You must have me confused
With someone else

I turn and head to the sofa
But Carl and the guy
In the Transformers jumper
Have gone to a back room
(This is a classy party)
And I am left
Alone
With men whose names
I cannot accurately remember

Scene Two

ANTHONY
Two days later
I'd sobered up
Told my counsellor
A relapse
A minor relapse at the weekend
A well-timed relapse is useful
For quieting the sound

Sound.

> COUNSELLOR
> Can you describe it for me?

ANTHONY (*shouting to be heard*)
It sounds like the ocean
Or a ticking time bomb

The sound stops.

> COUNSELLOR
> Might it be connected
> To your fear of seeing Jonathan this week?

ANTHONY
No that's going forward
Full-steam ahead

Which is why I find myself on Wednesday evening
Outside a flat on the Harringay Ladder
Waiting for someone to answer the door

Sobriety means that I had time
To contemplate the incident in Willesden Green
On Monday afternoon
Behind my desk in the British Library

> PLACARD
> Anthony Guest
> Assistant Curator of Ephemera

ANTHONY
(I have crossed out the word Assistant)

PLACARD
Anthony Guest
~~Assistant~~ Curator of Ephemera

ANTHONY
I re-read the headline

NEWSPAPER
The body of George Carnick
Twenty, of Dollis Hill
Discovered by dog walker

ANTHONY
I scan down the page
I read the interview with the dog walker

GENE
I approached the body
At first I thought he had been exercising
And taken a turn for the worse

ANTHONY
And a bit further on

GENE
But then I saw he wasn't breathing
And his right hand was rigid around a bottle
I called the police immediately

ANTHONY
'His right hand'
This detail unsettles me
George was useless with his right hand
His left hand however

I push the thought to the back of my mind
What happened in Willesden Green
Was a hallucination
That's all

JONATHAN
Anthony

ANTHONY
Jonathan

JONATHAN
So good of you to come
You look

ANTHONY
Older?

JONATHAN
I didn't expect you to make it

ANTHONY
Happy birthday
Here

JONATHAN
Cufflinks
You remembered

ANTHONY
Of course

Jonathan has a collection
Custom-made
All capital *J*s in various fonts
Palatino Linotype
Baskerville
These are in Centaur

JONATHAN
You shouldn't have

ANTHONY
I shouldn't have

In the intervening three years since we broke up
I had turned down several of Jonathan's invitations
The first to his book launch at Gay's the Word

JONATHAN
7 p.m.
Wine reception to follow
RSVP by 16 March
PS I've forgiven you for what you've done
Let's try to be friends?

ANTHONY
I ignored this one
He didn't want to forgive me
He simply wanted me along for comparison's sake
A reminder of his old life
And how far removed from it he was
While I of course
Couldn't get promoted
And was under constant performance review
Even though I never let what happened at the weekend
Interfere with my working life

But his invitation for his twenty-sixth birthday party
Seemed an appropriate time to make amends

    JONATHAN
    You're looking well

ANTHONY
So are you

    JONATHAN
    Come in

ANTHONY
Jonathan leads me inside the flat
He is turning twenty-six
But his friends are much older
I don't recognise any of them from the days
When we were together
This is perhaps what happens
When one becomes a journalist
Has a book deal
Writes about one's narrow escape
From a troubled past

    JONATHAN
    Everyone
    This is Anthony

ANTHONY
They greet me like a houseplant
They have no pot for

    JACK (THE ELDER)
    I'm Jack

JACK (THE YOUNGER)
Also Jack

EDWARD
Edward

HENRY
Henry

CHRISTOPHER
Christopher
(Never Chris)

WILLIAM
William
(Never Will)

FELIX
Felix

JONATHAN (*calling*)
Nibbles are on the table

ANTHONY
They are respectively

JACK (THE ELDER)
A popular academic

JACK (THE YOUNGER)
I'm a student
At Oxford

EDWARD
A civil servant

HENRY
Also a civil servant

EDWARD
We were recently in the news

WILLIAM
A food critic

CHRISTOPHER
I'm with the *Guardian*

FELIX
Children's television

ANTHONY
They have an air of respectability about them
But with the exception of the younger Jack
I am aware that they are here
Because Jonathan is turning twenty-six
While they
Like me
Are starting to discover flecks of grey in their hair
Looking in the mirror and finding
Skin with that stretched quality it achieves
Before breaking into wrinkles

Over a starter of

>JONATHAN
>Blackened cabbage with pine nut
>Here's the balsamic glaze

ANTHONY
I try conversing with the popular academic
(He is one of the Jacks)
(There are two)
He must be aware of me
Of my role in Jonathan's story
To avoid awkwardness
I ask if he's heard of George's body on the tumulus

>JACK (THE ELDER)
>*Tumulus*
>From the Latin meaning *mound*
>Legend says it's the burial place
>Of an ancient Celtic tribe
>Or the grave of Boudica

ANTHONY
Boudica?

>JACK (THE ELDER)
>Also pronounced Boudicea
>My next book is on the subject

ANTHONY
Later in the evening
After Jonathan has turned his eyes away from me again
As he serves the main course

JONATHAN
Duck *à l'orange*

ANTHONY
I ask Henry and Edward the same question

HENRY
No never heard anything

EDWARD
That's not true
We read it in the *Ham and High*

HENRY
Of course
Tragic

EDWARD
Tragic that
After we've all fought so hard
To maintain our sense of self-preservation
To have another epidemic in our midst

HENRY
A spiritual epidemic

EDWARD
Is such a shame

HENRY
Did you know him?

EDWARD
Was he among your
Set?

HENRY
Must've worked bloody hard
Getting himself across the Heath
With all those drugs in his body

ANTHONY
I look at them in their complementary
(But not matching)
Bow ties
They have a point
The quantities of *G* necessary to kill George

Would have rendered him immobile first
Meaning that he either consumed it on the tumulus
On the spot where he died
Or somewhere else
Somewhere near the Heath
And somebody carried
(Dragged?)
His body to the tumulus

Over a dessert of

>JONATHAN
>Peruvian dark-chocolate mousse
>Layered with sea-salt caramel
>Topped with Armagnac-soaked cherries
>And a served on a spun-sugar nest
>With a lozenge of champagne jelly

ANTHONY
I ask the television presenter Felix
Who says he eats so quickly

>FELIX
>Because the other boys at Eton
>Always stole my food

ANTHONY
If he has heard of the incident

>FELIX
>On the Heath?
>Of course
>It was my Aunt Genevieve
>Walking her dog
>Who found him
>Here's her number if you'd like to contact her

ANTHONY
Later still
As Jonathan leans closely against
An older journalist
His hand on the man's knee
I recall what he said to me when we broke up

>JONATHAN
>I don't feel safe around you any more

ANTHONY
Which was preposterous
I am always safe
Always in control

The younger Jack walks by
His eyes meet mine
I follow him to the terrace
I am about to kiss him when

> JONATHAN
> Anthony
> Anthony are you out here?

ANTHONY
Jonathan has stepped onto the terrace
His face does not move
It is here that I should explain
That by 'younger' Jack
I mean Jack is nineteen
Reading Medieval History at Oxford
He also happens to be
Jonathan's younger cousin

> JONATHAN
> Jack
> Will you give us a moment?

ANTHONY
Cigarette?

> JONATHAN
> I quit two years ago

ANTHONY
There's no need to be upset

> JONATHAN
> He's my cousin

ANTHONY
Don't take this the wrong way but
He's more handsome than you were at his age

> JONATHAN
> You're in my home
> On my birthday

And what's this I hear about you
Going around talking about bodies on the tumulus
Telling everyone who'd listen
That you slept with
Whatever his name was

ANTHONY
George
Yes
Tragic isn't it
I've never had a lover die on me before
This isn't the eighties

> JONATHAN
> People will talk

ANTHONY
Isn't that what you wanted?
Inviting me here in the first place

> JONATHAN
> I don't know why I invited you
> It's clear nothing has changed in your life
> Still going to parties
> And obsessing over teenagers
> You need to grow up
> Why do you care so much about George anyway?

ANTHONY
You sound jealous
Or like you knew him

> JONATHAN
> Me?
> No
> Never heard of him

ANTHONY
Even after three years
It's easy to tell when you're lying

> JONATHAN
> I think it's time you left
> You're embarrassing yourself
> And stay away from Jack
> I don't want you putting him in danger

ANTHONY
What Jack chooses to do is his own business
I would never put him in any danger
I am always careful
Always in control

> JONATHAN
> If that's what you need to tell yourself
> In order to sleep at night
> That's your business
> Goodnight Anthony

ANTHONY
Goodnight Jonathan

He leaves the terrace
And I am left alone
The glow of the moonlight
Hazy in the smoke from my cigarette

Scene Three

Anthony's flat.

ANTHONY
I tell Jack that I live in West Hampstead
But we alight at Kilburn Station
Because it's a closer walk

> JACK (THE YOUNGER)
> I'd like to put my arm in yours

ANTHONY
Maybe when we're alone

We reach my flat
I lead Jack down the long entrance hallway
Lined with books

Some guys are into me
Because I live alone
Or because I have a steady job
George was into me

GEORGE
Because you feel like a solid piece of earth

ANTHONY
He
(Like me)
Was estranged from his family

But Jack
Like Jonathan before him
Is into me
Because I am the
~~Assistant~~ Curator of Ephemera
At the British Library
Jack will return to Oxford
And tell his best friend
On his medieval history course

> JACK (THE YOUNGER)
> This guy I hooked up with
> He works at the BL

ANTHONY
He will sit in a tutorial
And mention offhandedly

> JACK (THE YOUNGER)
> Oh yes
> I know someone at the BL

ANTHONY
I show him my collection
Of poetry pamphlets from the late eighties

Here
Read the dedications

> JACK (THE YOUNGER)
> 'To the dearly departed'

ANTHONY
And

> JACK (THE YOUNGER)
> 'For Jon, Brian, Devan, and Arnie
> And those who have gone before
> From one who will shortly follow'

ANTHONY
I lead him to the kitchen

Anything to drink?

> JACK (THE YOUNGER)
> Just water

ANTHONY
I pour him a glass
And set it on my mid-century dining table
I open the fridge
And pull out a carton of cloudy apple juice
Bought from the West Hampstead farmers' market
I take out my own syringe and a glass
I measure carefully

Would you like some?

> JACK (THE YOUNGER)
> I've never done it before
> My cousin told me not to

ANTHONY
It will make us feel
Like live wires plugged into the same circuit
And crucially
Crucially
I find it helps with the

Sound.

ANTHONY *drinks.*

He mixes another.

> JACK (THE YOUNGER)
> You have it too?

ANTHONY
Mine sounds like the ocean
Or a ticking time bomb

> JACK (THE YOUNGER)
> Mine sounds like

Sound.

ANTHONY (*struggling to be heard*)
What?

> JACK (THE YOUNGER) (*shouting*)
> Buzzing
> Or a metal door being dragged across asphalt

ANTHONY *holds out the glass*.

The sound stops.

ANTHONY
Drink it all in one go
Otherwise you'll taste it

JACK *drinks*.

It is while I am watching Jack drink
His prominent Adam's apple bobbing up and down
In the same way Jonathan's does
That something triggers in my brain
Something remembered

> GENE
> At first I thought he had been exercising

ANTHONY
I look at the solution I have just mixed
My heart begins to race

> JACK (THE YOUNGER)
> It tastes awful

ANTHONY
I pull out the slip of paper Felix gave me
I have a hunch

Just a minute

I dial
While I wait for an answer
I keep my eyes on Jack
Watching for signs that the drug has taken effect
Watching him turn from bone into cartilage

> GENE
> Hello?

ANTHONY
Genevieve?
This is Anthony
I'm a friend of your nephew
Felix told me you had an unfortunate experience
Last week
While walking your dog

> GENE
> Hastings
> Yes
> We had passed through the copse
> Connecting Parliament Hill
> With the tumulus
> When Hastings bolts forward
> And begins licking a man slouched over
> I call Hastings off and approach slowly
> I try to shake him but there's no response

ANTHONY
You said in the paper
You thought he had been exercising
Why exercise?

> GENE
> Because of the bottle
> It was one of those sports drinks
> Leviathan
> Linocaine

ANTHONY
Lucozade?

> GENE
> That's the one
> Bright orange

ANTHONY
I hang up the phone
Jack looks at me strangely
Happy
Blissful

JACK (THE YOUNGER)
It's true
The sound has disappeared

ANTHONY
It is now starting to have an effect on me too
Here is a nineteen-year-old in front of me
And I am not yet thirty-three

I begin to loosen Jack's tie
Remove a handsome silver tie clip
Unbutton his shirt
I lean in to kiss Jack's mouth
He speaks
But it is not him speaking

GEORGE
Anthony

ANTHONY
George

GEORGE
You discovered

ANTHONY
Yes

GEORGE
You know I didn't overdose
You know it was murder
The missing necklace
The bottle in the wrong hand
But most of all
Gamma-Butyrolactone
In a mixture I never would have
Could have
Drunk

ANTHONY
The bottle was a plant

GEORGE
Yes it was

ANTHONY
You were murdered

GEORGE
Yes
Yes I was

ANTHONY
What do you want me to do?

GEORGE
I need my necklace back
I need it desperately

ANTHONY
And then what?

GEORGE
That's up to you

ANTHONY
And why should I help you?
So what if you were murdered?
You don't mean anything to me

GEORGE
We both know that's not true
We both know that I was becoming
More than just a

ANTHONY
My feelings were under control
Now if you don't mind
I'd like to speak to Jack again
Give me Jack back

No response.

I said give me Jack back

GEORGE
No
Not until you promise

ANTHONY
Fine
But I want something in return

GEORGE
What?

ANTHONY
Make it go away

> GEORGE
> Make what go away?

Sound.

They listen to the sound.

The sound stops.

ANTHONY
Make it go away
For good

Pause.

> GEORGE
> Okay
> When you find my necklace

ANTHONY
Okay

ACT TWO

Scene One

A police station.

ANTHONY
On Friday afternoon
On a half-day from work
I am standing in a police station
I am wearing a trenchcoat and fedora
Looking the part helps focus the mind

> CALLUM
> Can I help you?

ANTHONY
I'd like to report a crime

> CALLUM
> Is it currently in progress?

ANTHONY
No

> CALLUM
> Then have you called 101?

ANTHONY
No I –

> CALLUM
> Then I suggest you use the phone in the lobby

ANTHONY
But I

ANTHONY*'s phone rings.*

> CALLUM
> Sir the sign outside
> Clearly states that all mobile phones
> Are to be turned off before entering
> And if you don't mind my saying

It's difficult to see you
With that hat on

ANTHONY
Yes I am aware that –

It's Jack
This is the third time he's called
I made the mistake of letting him spend the night
Seeing as it was so late
By the time we were finished

    CALLUM
    Sir if you could put your phone on silent

ANTHONY *silences his phone.*

ANTHONY
The officer looks at me smugly
Like he's taken a very satisfying shit

Now as I was saying
I'd like to report a crime

    CALLUM
    It's best to route all information through 101

ANTHONY
I don't mean to be rude
But a boy is dead
A young man
Not much younger than I am
(I am not yet thirty-three)

    CALLUM
    I don't care what his age is
    The information needs to go through 101

ANTHONY
He died on the Heath
On the tumulus
I'm his boyfriend

I assume a small lie won't hurt
There's a certain moral authority
That comes with saying *boyfriend*

CALLUM
Martin

MARTIN (*offstage*)
What is it Callum?

CALLUM
A man wants to report a crime

MARTIN (*offstage*)
Has he phoned 101?

CALLUM
It's about the guy
On the tumulus
This man claims to be
His boyfriend

Enter MARTIN.

MARTIN
Nice hat

MARTIN *gives* CALLUM *a look*.

I am the LGBTQIA-plus liaison officer
We were unaware the victim had a partner
May I take your name?

ANTHONY
Anthony
Anthony Guest

MARTIN
And you are the victim's boyfriend?

ANTHONY
That is correct

MARTIN
And what was your boyfriend's name?

ANTHONY
George

MARTIN
And his surname?

ANTHONY
Oh
Um

> MARTIN
> Sir?

ANTHONY
Carney

> MARTIN
> Excuse me?

ANTHONY
Carnick
George Carnick

MARTIN *indicates to* CALLUM.

CALLUM *exits*.

> MARTIN
> And how long had you two been

ANTHONY
If you'll excuse me
Are you implying that

> MARTIN
> I'm only asking
> As a matter of course

ANTHONY
Excuse me
Martin
But my *boyfriend*
Is dead
Not just dead
Murdered

> MARTIN
> Are you aware
> That the cause of death was an overdose?

ANTHONY
I am
But my *boyfriend*
Had an allergy to Lucozade

He never would have taken *G* with it
Something only I
(His boyfriend)
Would know
And given that the amount of *G* in his system
Was enough to kill him
He couldn't have walked to the tumulus either
Someone must have carried him there
Someone else is involved
A murder

I give my coat a little flick
And wait for the applause

Enter CALLUM, *who holds a clear plastic bag and reads from a label.*

> CALLUM
> Carnick
> Comma
> George
> 24 Yewfield Road

CALLUM *dumps the contents of the bag onto a table.*

ANTHONY
Have you checked everything for DNA?

> MARTIN
> We only devote resources
> To those kinds of investigations
> When the cause isn't obvious

> CALLUM
> It's very clear what happened

ANTHONY
Did you test anything?

> MARTIN
> We confirmed that the bottle
> Contains GBL

ANTHONY
And Lucozade
Which he doesn't drink

MARTIN
There are many reasons
Why he might drink from that (*sound*)

ANTHONY
Excuse me?

MARTIN
There are many reasons
Why he might drink from that bottle

ANTHONY
It gave him a rash
Did he have a rash?

MARTIN
Mr Guest

ANTHONY
Did you check?
Did you check if his body had a rash?

MARTIN
Mr Guest really

ANTHONY
It made him vomit
Was he found with vomit on him?
If it made him vomit
How could he have kept it down?

MARTIN
Mr Guest
Would you like to sit?

ANTHONY
I would not like to sit

MARTIN
Mr Guest
Take a deep breath

ANTHONY
I want to fight them
I want to

MARTIN
Mr (*sound*)

ANTHONY
Excuse me?

MARTIN
Let us try to explain

CALLUM
Young men

MARTIN
Young gay men
Like your boyfriend

CALLUM
Three a month

MARTIN
One every twelve days

CALLUM
Overdosing

MARTIN
They're not careful

CALLUM
They think they're invincible

MARTIN
Their friends

CALLUM
Their so-called friends

MARTIN
Don't call an ambulance

CALLUM
But don't want a body in their home

MARTIN
Who wants a body in their home?

CALLUM
So bodies are left

MARTIN
Discarded

CALLUM
The kerb

MARTIN
The (*sound*)

ANTHONY
What did you say?
I'm having trouble

MARTIN
The tumulus

ANTHONY
But the bottle in his hand
It's the wrong hand
It's

MARTIN
(*sound*) to terms with the loss
Of a loved one is (*sound*)

ANTHONY (*speaking over*)
I'm sorry
I don't understand [what you're saying]

MARTIN
I'm sure your (*sound*)
Was a very (*sound*) person
But he is part of a pattern

CALLUM
Young men

MARTIN
Young (*sound*) men
Like your (*sound*)

CALLUM
(*sound*) a (*sound*)

ANTHONY
I don't

MARTIN
(*sound*)

ANTHONY
I can't

CALLUM
(*sound*)

ANTHONY
Stop it

MARTIN
(*sound*)

ANTHONY
Stop it
Stop speaking

CALLUM
(*sound*)

ANTHONY
I need a

MARTIN
(*sound*)

CALLUM
(*sound*)

MARTIN
Body in their (*sound*)

ANTHONY *frantically pats himself down, searching for a cigarette.*

He tries lighting up.

CALLUM
No (*sound*)

MARTIN
Mr (*sound*)
(*sound*) cannot (*sound*)

ANTHONY
No I need a

CALLUM
Mr (*sound*)

MARTIN
This is your last (*sound*)

ANTHONY
Please
Let me

    CALLUM
    Come with (*sound*)

ANTHONY
Please
Let me

The OFFICERS *take hold of* ANTHONY.

The sound is now constant.

The OFFICERS *throw* ANTHONY *outside.*

    CALLUM
    (*sound*)

    MARTIN
    (*sound*)

The OFFICERS *turn.*

The OFFICERS *exit.*

ANTHONY, *alone.*

Pause.

He smokes.

He tries to catch his breath.

ANTHONY'*s phone rings.*

He smokes and lets it ring as the sound slowly fades.

    VOICEMAIL
    The person you are trying to call
    Is currently unavailable
    Please leave a message after the tone

Tone.

    JACK (THE YOUNGER)
    Hi Anthony
    It's me Jack
    Wondered if you wanted to see a film tonight?
    Or go to the theatre?

Or an exhibition?
Let me know?
I had a good time earlier this week?
You know?
And like?
If you wanted to?
Like?
Do that stuff again?
I'd like?
Be into that?
Because it was like?
The sex was like?
Like?
Like being hit by a bus
A really
Happy
Bus
Okay phone me bye

Pause.

ANTHONY
Maybe they're right
There are any number of reasons
George would have a bottle of Lucozade
In his right hand
Maybe George's appearance was all
A hallucination
Maybe

But that's when something happens
Something I do not expect

The ping of a text message.

ANTHONY *picks up his phone.*

I read it

TEXT
BACK OFF FAGGOTT

Faggott
Spelt with two *T*s
Someone doesn't want me investigating
I'm hitting a nerve

Scene Two

A flat in Dollis Hill.

ANTHONY
So this is the bed

> OWEN
> Yeah

ANTHONY
It's pretty big

> OWEN
> Yeah

ANTHONY
Which side was his?

> OWEN
> The left
> As you're facing it

ANTHONY
How much a month?

> OWEN
> Two-eight-five plus bills
> Pretty good for London yeah?
> Found it on SpareRoom
> How much do you pay?

ANTHONY
More than that
But I have my own bed

I am in a run-down house
In Dollis Hill
Owen
(George's bedmate)
Is (I think) older than I expected
But it's hard to tell
Straight men are allowed
To let themselves go

> OWEN
> So were you like his boyfriend or something?
> 'Cause I don't remember him mentioning one

ANTHONY
We got together once or twice

> OWEN
> In the bed?

ANTHONY
I smile at Owen
A straight man's imagination
Is always his worst enemy

Had he been here long?

> OWEN
> About six months
> I mean nothing happened between us
> 'Cause I'm not you know
> Like that

ANTHONY
Sure

> OWEN
> I have a girlfriend

ANTHONY
Okay

> OWEN
> Well like
> I did at the time

ANTHONY
How did you find out he was dead?

> OWEN
> I hadn't seen him in a few days
> Which wasn't unusual
> 'Cause he slept away some nights
> I got the impression
> He sometimes did that for money?
> But then he didn't turn up
> And rent was due the next day
> And we were like
> Where the hell is George?
> And then an officer comes to the door

And tells us he's dead
And we're like
Does that mean we still have to pay the rent?

ANTHONY
His story intrigues me
It was always clear that George had run away
It was something we had in common
But I never enquired too closely
What he did for a living

What made you think he slept with men for money?

OWEN
It's that one time
Look
I'm not like you and he are
Understand?
But like one time he came home late
And he got into bed
And I could feel the mattress
Shudder
Softly
And he was drawing these shallow breaths
And I realised he was crying
And I didn't want to say anything
'Cause I didn't want to embarrass him
So I rolled over toward him
And kinda like put my arm around him
And just like
Held him
He didn't say anything
But then after a moment
He reached onto the bedside table
Fumbled with his wallet
And pulled out a tenner
He held it up to me and said

I'll give you a tenner
If you hold me until I fall asleep

ANTHONY
What did you do?

OWEN
I took the tenner
And held him until he fell asleep
So that's why I think he was used to
Associating money and
And

ANTHONY
He's looking for a word that means
The closeness of two men
But he does not know a word
For that kind of closeness
Of live wires plugged into the same circuit
A thought strikes me
Something my counsellor said

COUNSELLOR
How do you feel if I suggest
Practising learning to experience
Male-male affection
Outside the context of being high?

ANTHONY
Here was an opportunity to practise

Show me

OWEN
What?

ANTHONY
Show me how you held him
I need to place myself in his headspace
In order to think

It sounds plausible

OWEN
I don't

ANTHONY
Your bedmate was dead on the tumulus
And all you were concerned about
Was the rent
You owe him this

OWEN *relents*.

OWEN *begins to lie down*.

Wait

> OWEN
> What?

ANTHONY
Did you have your shirt on?

OWEN *gives* ANTHONY *a look*.

OWEN *takes off his shirt*.

OWEN *and* ANTHONY *lie down*.

OWEN *places his arm around* ANTHONY.

Like this?

> OWEN
> Yes

ANTHONY
It's true
I am able to think better
If George slept with men for money
(He never asked me for any)
Then perhaps someone hired him for his youth
Someone growing older
Someone already old
Older than not-yet thirty-three
With disposable income

It is as I am having these thoughts
That I try to remember the last time I was held
It must have happened one weekend at some point
Surely
To feel made of cartilage
To feel like live wires plugged into the same circuit
Certainly we must have touched
Must have held
But I cannot remember being held

Cannot remember the contact
Only the desire for it

That's enough

> OWEN
> Okay

ANTHONY
Let me go

> OWEN
> I've let you go

ANTHONY
I said let me go

ANTHONY *takes a moment to recover.*

Thanks for your time
One last thing
His necklace isn't here is it?
It wasn't found on him

OWEN
The eye?
No
We put everything in the box in the corner
You're welcome to look through it

ANTHONY
Thanks
I'll see myself out

Exit OWEN.

I move toward the box
Bend down and rifle through
What's immediately apparent is the lack of photographs
Memories
A handful of books
A meagre collection of clothes
And there
In the corner of the box
An answer

ANTHONY *picks up a small silver cufflink.*

A small silver cufflink
Custom-made
The letter *J*
In Garamond font
The one I gave to Jonathan
Three years ago for his birthday

Scene Three

ANTHONY
I race back to Dollis Hill Station
London spread out beneath me
Like a sinking ship whose lights haven't yet gone out
I have half a dozen texts on my phone
Most (I suspect) from Jack

> JACK (THE YOUNGER)
> Anthony let's hang out okay?
>
> Anthony I want to try it again okay?
>
> Anthony why aren't you speaking to me?
>
> Anthony?
>
> Anthony?

ANTHONY
But my mind is preoccupied
Jonathan knows more than he's told me
How did one of his cufflinks
End up in the remains of George's life?
It is as I contemplate this question
That I hear a noise behind me

Footsteps.

I am suddenly aware
Of how dark London is
On its hills

Of how alone
You can be in a city

Hello?

ANTHONY *turns and continues to walk.*

The footsteps start again.

ANTHONY *turns.*

Hello who's there?

The footsteps stop.

ANTHONY *continues.*

I press on
Swearing never again
To travel beyond zone two

The footsteps.

George?
George is that you?

ANTHONY *walks faster.*

The footsteps chase.

A fear starts to grow within me
I am reminded of all the times
I have been chased
Had sticks thrown at me
Spit spat at me on the Tube
I feel my heart beating faster
I feel control slipping

ANTHONY *begins to run.*

The footsteps chase.

In the distance, the sound.

I am reminded of a time
When I was sixteen
Men coming toward me
Jeering
Threatening
And then the attack

But the memory means that
When the blow comes
I am ready for it

Out of the darkness, a punch.

ANTHONY *blocks the punch.*

A man in a mask.

A struggle.

A fight.

ANTHONY *may be overpowered, but* ANTHONY *is stronger than he appears.*

Finally, ANTHONY, *triumphant.*

He pulls off the mask.

JONATHAN.

ANTHONY
Jonathan
I suspected it was you

> JONATHAN
> Anthony

Scene Four

Jonathan's home.

ANTHONY
I am standing in Jonathan's kitchen
Watching as he holds an icepack to his forehead
He once told me
That his sound

> *Sound.*

> JONATHAN (*shouting to be heard*)
> Sounds like a nail scratching across glass
> Or ceramics shattering

The sound stops.

ANTHONY
I wonder if that
Is what is going through his head now

I assume you hired him

    JONATHAN
    Yes

ANTHONY *holds out the cufflink.*

ANTHONY
On more than one occasion?

    JONATHAN
    I wondered where that had gone

ANTHONY
How much did you pay for George's services?

    JONATHAN
    Eight hundred pounds

ANTHONY
Why did you feel the need to pay?

    JONATHAN
    I wasn't by myself

ANTHONY
Oh

I recall the journalist
Whose knee Jonathan rested his hand upon
At his party

And I take it
From the fact that you
Went to extreme measures
To stop my investigations
Faggot is spelled with one *T* by the way
That you hired him

    JONATHAN
    Yes
    We did

But he left by seven
Very much alive

ANTHONY
Do you have proof?
Can anyone vouch for your whereabouts
For the entire evening?

No response.

Jonathan I asked
If anyone saw you later that night

No response.

Jonathan were you

    JONATHAN
    I went to a party afterward

ANTHONY
What sort of party?

    JONATHAN
    None of your business

ANTHONY
It's a straightforward question

    JONATHAN
    I'm not your boyfriend any more
    I don't have to answer

ANTHONY
I would hate to have to go to the police
To inform them I found someone who slept with George
On the night he died

I refrain of course from telling Jonathan
That the police have no interest in the case

    JONATHAN
    Yes other people can vouch for my whereabouts

ANTHONY
How many others?

Beat.

Four?

Beat.

A dozen?

Beat.

Where was this party?

> JONATHAN
> Archway

ANTHONY
Was Wandering Joe there?

JONATHAN *nods.*

How long did you go?

> JONATHAN
> Thirty-six hours

ANTHONY
The news sends shockwaves through me
But also a grim kind of triumph
For the last three years
Jonathan has made a career out of
Being a reformed character
News articles
Self-righteous blog posts
Television interviews
A book

When did you start again?

> JONATHAN
> I haven't started again
> I'm not going back to it
> It was a one-off
> A temporary relapse
> But if I have to explain my whereabouts
> That evening
> Because you've been asking questions
> Then everything I've worked for
> Will be gone
> So please
> Let this go

ANTHONY
Why should I?

>JONATHAN
>Anthony
>I know you're upset
>I know you're angry that I broke it off

ANTHONY
Didn't just break it off
Dragged my life into the open
They won't promote me at work
All of my friends have left me

>JONATHAN
>What did you expect?
>I couldn't keep going like that
>It was dangerous
>It is dangerous
>
>Do you know
>The only way I can recall that night
>Is in my dreams?
>Figures and
>Hands
>And

ANTHONY
I wasn't going to let anything happen to you

I am in control
I am always in control

>JONATHAN
>Are you sure?
>Were you even aware of what was happening?

ANTHONY
Occasionally in hour thirty-three
Or forty-one
Someone has had too much
The dosage just a bit off
Two millilitres
When you should've had
One point five
The feeling is funny

Instead of cartilage
You feel like
Lead
You go under

> JONATHAN
> They touched me Anthony
> You let them touch me

ANTHONY
It's not a big deal
It happens
It's something you expect
Almost something
You sign up for
Just by being present

> JONATHAN
> I could've been overdosing
> Dying
> But instead you watched
> You watched them do that to me

ANTHONY *turns*.

> Anthony

ANTHONY *does not respond*.

> Anthony please
> I need help
> I don't want this
> Taking over my life again
> I'm seeing the counsellor tomorrow
> If you need to find out
> What happened to George
> That's fine
> Maybe you were starting to like him
> Even have feelings for him

ANTHONY
Don't be ridiculous

> JONATHAN
> But please
> Please

>Leave me out of it
>I'm barely holding it together
>Going public will push me over the edge

JONATHAN *rifles through his pocket*.

>Here
>Take this
>I don't want it

ANTHONY
He holds out a small glass bottle
With an eyedropper top
I know what's inside

>JONATHAN
>Take it from me Anthony
>Please

ANTHONY
I look at it
I wonder how loud the sound in his head is
I know how loud it is in mine

Sound.

Fine
Fine I'll let you go

>JONATHAN
>Thank you

ANTHONY
I look at Jonathan
One last time
Then I walk out of his house
And shut the door behind me

At the gate
I consider opening the glass bottle
With the eyedropper top
And tipping the contents
Onto the concrete
But instead
I find myself
On Green Lanes
Buying a small carton of apple juice

In the darkness of the Haringey Passage
I drip the contents of the glass bottle in

One drop
Two drops
Three drops

Eyedroppers are hard to judge
I chug
Five minutes later
I am outside Jonathan's front door
My body feeling like cartilage
Wanting Jonathan to open the door
So that I can tell him
Everything will be okay
That we can feel connected
Live wires plugged into the same circuit
That I'm sorry for what happened that night
That I won't be out of control again
That I am conscientious
Orderly
That people who get near me
Don't end up hurt
Don't end up dead
That I can make it right
I can put things back in order
If he would just tell me
More about George
Where George went to later that night
Then may be I can find out
Who killed George
And everything will be okay
If he would
Just
Answer
The
Fucking
Door

The door opens.

GEORGE
Anthony

ANTHONY
George
Where's Jonathan?

GEORGE
He can't come to the door right now

ANTHONY
I want to speak to Jonathan

GEORGE
There's been a development

ANTHONY
Please
Give me back Jonathan

GEORGE
Someone would like to talk to you

ANTHONY
Who?

JACK (THE YOUNGER)
Anthony?
Anthony it's me
Jack

ANTHONY
What are you doing here?

JACK (THE YOUNGER)
George said you were helping him
Find his necklace

ANTHONY
George is dead

JACK (THE YOUNGER)
Can you help me too?
My silver tie clip is missing

Scene Five

Hampstead Heath.

ANTHONY
I am in an Uber
Willing the driver to go faster

Let me out here

I hurl out of the vehicle
The southern entrance to the Heath
A black vastness in front of me
I fear that
Like the ocean
I might drown in it

I make my way past the gate
Then up the steady incline
That leads past the first of the ponds
I consider that Jack might not be there
That this is all in my head
It's likely
(I tell myself)
That it was simply another hallucination
Or lingering guilt
For not returning Jack's texts
Even though the last one he sent to me said

    JACK (THE YOUNGER)
    I'll find some on my own

ANTHONY
I should know better
Than to get involved with someone so young
I keep telling myself
My next hook-up will be with someone my age
Someone appropriate
Someone I might have something in common with
But turns out I'm not so good at saying no to myself

I enter the small wood
Where the road forks
To the right
Parliament Hill
To the left

The path to the tumulus
I veer toward the left
Aware how quiet
How threatening the silence is
In the corner of my eye
On the path to the right
I can make out the figure of a man
Moving quickly away
I break out of the wood
To the grassy expanse
With its view of Highgate
And there
In the distance
The tumulus

I walk slowly forward
As I draw closer to the tumulus
I try to make out any shapes
Any bodies
But all I can see
Are the park benches
Perhaps this is all in my head after all

I flick on the light on my phone
And scan the area
I have reached the top side of the tumulus now
Close to where George was found
Jack's body doesn't appear to be here
I breathe a sigh of relief

I sit

It's all been in my head
George
Jack
An investigation
The police are right
I should give this up
George isn't my responsibility
He should have been more careful
Showed better judgment

I turn to read the bench inscription

PERCY
In loving memory of
Percy Holloway
1965–1988

ANTHONY
Twenty-three years old
And not difficult to guess
The cause of death
I wonder what his sound
Sounded like
Perhaps the crunching of bones

PERCY
(*sound*)

ANTHONY
Or the gnawing of rats

PERCY
(*sound*)

ANTHONY
It is as I am contemplating Percy
And his short-lived life
That I notice in the underbrush
Something that looks like
A bare branch
Or a small log
But as my eyes adjust to the dark
I realise

Sound.

A rigid hand

Sound.

I follow the hand
Up along its arm
And then perceive
The body it is connected to

Sound.

Oh fuck

JACK*'s body.*

Oh fuck fuck fuck fuck fuck fuck

ANTHONY *shines his phone light on* JACK*'s body.*

ANTHONY *checks the body for signs of life.*

There are none.

Jack
Jack wake up

Then ANTHONY *notices a Lucozade bottle in* JACK*'s hand.*

A Lucozade bottle
It's not all in my head
Someone is killing young men
Very young men
The kind of men I am attracted to
The police are right
There is a pattern
But not the one they were looking for

I try to take deep breaths
I can hear it approaching

Sound.

I try to calm down
I try to

    OFFICER A
    Stop
    Police
    Stay where you are!

ANTHONY
Shit
Shit shit shit

The cops already know
Someone has already been here
Already informed them
My prints are everywhere
There's no way this doesn't look suspicious

The sound grows louder still.

OFFICER B
Stop
Police!

ANTHONY
I have no choice
I run

Scene Six

ANTHONY
I run
I run and run
I look for familiar landmarks
But I am lost
I cannot get my bearings
The Heath is too disorienting in the dark
There's a crashing sound in my head
I don't know what to do
I need to find a way out
I need connection
And crucially
Crucially

Sound.

I need the sound to stop
I find a copse
Huddle behind a tree

ANTHONY *pulls out his phone.*

On my phone the world populates
It's early Sunday morning in Hampstead
Messages ping

A
Hey man

B
Hey sexxxxxy

C
Whatup?

D
Playtime?

E
Whatcha into?

F
Chems?

A
I'm gonna break u

ANTHONY
Can I come over?

A
What RU looking 4?

ANTHONY
G
Tina
Meow
U got any?

A
What U got 2 offer?
U hot?
U hung?
Send pics

ANTHONY
I send pics
He blocks me

Sound.

B
Top or btm?

C
Can you accom?

D
Nice bod

    E
    U hung?

ANTHONY
No

Sound.

    B
    U close?

ANTHONY
No

Sound.

    C
    U looking?

ANTHONY
Yes

Sound.

    D
    U fit?

Sound.

    E
    U alright?

Sound.

ANTHONY
No
I am not alright
I want it to end
I want everything to end
Men
Death
Chems
Jonathan
George
Jack
The police
The sound

I want the sound to stop
But the sound
It grows and grows

The sound intensifies.

I feel overwhelmed
I am overwhelmed

The sound reaches a cacophony.

A crash.

Suddenly, a moment of silence.

> JOE
> Anthony?

ANTHONY
Who's this?

> JOE
> Wandering Joe
> You looking for a party?

ANTHONY
Yeah

> JOE
> Come over
> We're having a good time
> See

ANTHONY
He sends me a pic
Of him in the kitchen
His spreadsheet
Vials of liquids
And half a dozen guys
Crowded round
And then I see
One of them
Standing behind Joe
Only half his face is visible
I zoom in
There

Around his neck
A golden chain
A necklace
The eye
To ward off evil

    JOE
    Here's our location

ANTHONY
25 South Hill Park Gardens
A short walk to the Heath
And the tumulus

I'll be right over

ACT THREE

Scene One

A flat in Hampstead.

ANTHONY
There is a crowd
Eleven
Twelve of them
They are entering hour thirty-four
When the strain starts to show
I'm normally one of them
Along for the ride
The live wire plugged into the circuit
But to my sober self
Their appearance is shocking
They reek of cat piss
In the corner
Some of them are slamming

> G
> What do you have for us?

ANTHONY
Nothing on me

> G
> Then try elsewhere

ANTHONY
No wait
Joe invited me

G *considers.*

> G
> Dealer's coming round
> In twenty minutes
> You can load up then

ANTHONY
I look around
Desperate to find
The man in the necklace

Have you seen

> I
> What?

ANTHONY
Guy in a necklace
An eye
'To ward off evil'
He was here
In a photo

> I
> Dunno mate
> Put these on

Holds out a pair of shorts.

ANTHONY
He must be around here
I am aware
That I do not have a plan
I cannot call the police
Not without getting everyone here
In trouble

I wander from room to room

> J
> Hey you want some?

ANTHONY
No thanks
Not yet

> J
> Suit yourself

ANTHONY
I head into the kitchen
And there
Stood before me is Wandering Joe

With his spreadsheet
But even Joe
After thirty-four hours
Starts to lose the air of command

Joe?

> JOE
> Hey

ANTHONY
Joe I need to talk to you

> JOE
> You want some?

ANTHONY
No thanks
I'm looking for someone
Someone with a necklace
He was in the photo you sent

> JOE
> Photo?

ANTHONY
That you sent earlier
Joe I need you to focus
This guy
This guy have you seen him?

ANTHONY *holds out his phone.*

> JOE
> Dunno
> But here
> Try this

JOE *holds a glass to* ANTHONY*'s lips and tilts back*
ANTHONY*'s head, forcing* ANTHONY *to drink.*

ANTHONY
What the fuck?

> JOE
> What?
> You're here aren't you?

ANTHONY
How much was in that?

> JOE
> Not much
> I think
> You'll be fine
> You're an old pro

ANTHONY
Joe please
Concentrate
Do you recognise this guy?

> JOE
> That's me

ANTHONY
No the person behind you

> JOE
> He only has half a face
> What happened to the other half of his face?

ANTHONY
It's cropped out
But can you tell who it is?

> JOE
> It kind of looks like
> Looks like

ANTHONY
Who?

> JOE
> My neighbour

ANTHONY
Your neighbour?

> JOE
> Downstairs

ANTHONY
This is your house?

> JOE
> Got to live somewhere

ANTHONY
Where is he now?

>JOE
>Left I think
>Why?
>You like the look of him?
>Didn't realise he was your type
>But if you want to go to his
>Here's his key
>He gives it to me in case people
>Need a place to chill out

JOE *hands* ANTHONY *the key.*

>Have fun

Scene Two

The downstairs flat.

ANTHONY
I open the door to the flat
Inside is dark
No one appears at home
But the blinds are raised
And in the moonlight
Reflected off the Heath
I can see the contents

Books line shelves along two walls
Posters of exhibitions
Theatre shows
Mix with
Sketches of nude men
(They appear young)
(Very young)
Drawn from life

The John Lewis sofa
Looks ruffled
On a mid-century coffee table

Rest two empty glasses of red wine
At the bottom of one
A sludge
The residue of
Gamma-Butyrolactone
In its powdered form

I should look for the necklace
Make my time here short
My limbs are already starting to feel of cartilage
But as I scan the shelves
I become distracted by the collection
Several histories of the Heath
An entire section on cottaging
Another on the ponds
And then
A full row of books
Biographies
Of Boudica

Or Boudicea

Footsteps.

A key at the door.

Shit
I am in no condition to run
I hide the only place I can find
Behind the curtains

Enter JACK (THE ELDER), *wearing wellington boots, a coat
and scarf.*

JACK *switches on the lights.*

He looks around.

He wonders if his house has been disturbed.

I consider
Hidden though I am behind a curtain
That I did not bolt the door

> JACK (THE ELDER)
> Hello
> Hello who's in here?

JACK *looks around again.*

> Anyone here?
> Joe?

ANTHONY
If I hold very still
And don't say anything
Don't say that I'm feeling very scared
And that if he goes into the kitchen
Then perhaps I can slip out unnoticed

But one of the effects of the chems
Is saying exactly what you feel

I'm feeling very scared
But if you go into the kitchen
Then perhaps I can slip out unnoticed

> JACK (THE ELDER)
> Fucking hell
> Who are you?
> What are you doing in my flat?

ANTHONY
I was
Joe
I was upstairs and Joe
We ran out of
He sent me down to ask
If you had some

> JACK (THE ELDER)
> How did you get in?

ANTHONY
He gave me a key

> JACK (THE ELDER)
> I told him not to give
> The key to anybody

ANTHONY
It's hour thirty-four
His memory isn't as precise
As it should be

JACK (THE ELDER)
Excuse me but
Do I know you?
You sound familiar
Step into the light

ANTHONY
Really
I should just be on
Just be on my way

JACK (THE ELDER)
Step into the light
And take off that hat
Slowly

ANTHONY *obeys*.

You're

ANTHONY
Anthony
Anthony Guest

JACK (THE ELDER)
Jonathan's

ANTHONY
Ex
That's right
Coincidence
What a coincidence
Ending up here
And you're

JACK (THE ELDER)
Jack

ANTHONY
That's right
The popular academic

JACK (THE ELDER)
Yes

ANTHONY
One of the two Jacks at the party

At the mention of the second Jack
His face blanches

Sound.

I take a close look at him
Searching for the necklace
Or the silver tie clip
But they are not visible

You know
I couldn't help noticing
Your collection
It's impressive
I am an ~~Assistant~~ Curator
At the BL
I have knowledge of such things

>   JACK (THE ELDER)
>   Thanks
>   But it's late

ANTHONY
I notice now
That he is agitated
His hands shake
And he has a wild look in his eyes

Of course you must want to get some sleep
Having just come from the Heath

>   JACK (THE ELDER)
>   Excuse me?

ANTHONY
The wellingtons
And the coat and scarf
Do you often wander the Heath at night?
Sorry
That sounds suggestive
I don't mean to be
It's just that Joe gave me
I'm not sure what he gave me

>   JACK (THE ELDER)
>   Look it's very late

ANTHONY
Of course
Of course

>JACK (THE ELDER)
>I'd like you to leave

ANTHONY
Of course

>JACK (THE ELDER)
>Now

ANTHONY
He has grown more threatening
I have run out of ways
To keep him engaged
All I can offer is

ANTHONY *holds out the eyedropper bottle.*

ANTHONY
Do you want some?

>JACK (THE ELDER)
>Excuse me?

ANTHONY
We've run out upstairs
But I have a little left
Care to join?

>JACK (THE ELDER)
>I want to be left alone

ANTHONY
You seem stressed
(No offence)
Distracted
And if I may observe
You appear due for another hit
It will help with the sound
Yours seems particularly loud
At the moment

He stares at me
Like he is reading the same paragraph

Of a book
Over and over again

Do you have some apple juice?

> JACK (THE ELDER)
> I'll be right back

ANTHONY
He leaves for the kitchen

Suddenly I feel groggy
Unhinged

Sound.

I have no idea how much Joe gave me
And I have still not seen the necklace
I consider that maybe I have made a mistake
Instead of staying
I should leave
Wait until I am sober
Call the police
I open the front door of the flat

Sound.

> GEORGE
> Anthony

ANTHONY
George

> GEORGE
> Where are you going?

ANTHONY
I've made a mistake
I should leave
Wait until I am sober
Call the police

> GEORGE
> Will the police listen?

ANTHONY
What?

GEORGE
Will they even listen if you call?

ANTHONY
I'm not in a fit state
And I don't see the necklace
I should go

GEORGE
I can't let you leave
Until you find the necklace
Besides
This flat looks familiar
So many books on the shelves
And the sketches
Do you like the sketches on the wall?

Enter JACK.

JACK (THE ELDER)
No apple
But I have Lucozade
Oh
You're leaving

GEORGE
Who's that Anthony?
I feel I recognise him

ANTHONY
No
Sorry
Needed some fresh air
That's all

GEORGE
Go back inside Anthony

ANTHONY
Jack seems somehow calmer
The wellingtons have come off
And the coat and scarf
But the necklace
And the silver tie clip
Are still not visible

He places the Lucozade
On the coffee table
Along with a small glass

>JACK (THE ELDER)
>Strange
>Your turning up here
>Tonight

>GEORGE
>Yes it's coming back
>It's coming back to me Anthony

ANTHONY
Yes
Of all the places
Though I must say
I find it surprising
You
A popular academic
And I
An ~~assistant~~ curator
Brought together
By a small bottle of liquid

>GEORGE
>Be careful what he offers
>You to drink

ANTHONY
How did you start
If you don't mind my asking?

If there is one thing I have learned
From working at the BL
It is that academics
Love being asked questions
About themselves

>JACK (THE ELDER)
>Research
>For my new book
>More and more men on the Heath
>Talk about 'chems'
>About ways to make the sound go silent

    I was curious
    And having Joe

ANTHONY
Wandering Joe

    JACK (THE ELDER)
    For an upstairs neighbour
    Meant that one night
    When the sound
    Was particularly bad
    It was easy to ask
    If he had anything
    That could quiet it

    I had been suspicious
    Prudish
    I had read Jonathan's book
    Had heard
    Had even myself
    When I was younger
    (I am not yet forty-five)
    Taken substances
    But not a substance like this

    I have to be careful
    Of course

ANTHONY
We all have to be careful

    JACK (THE ELDER)
    Not to let

ANTHONY
Not to let

    JACK (THE ELDER)
    Not to let it get
    Out of control

ANTHONY
Your books
Are nicely alphabetised
By subject

JACK (THE ELDER)
Though sometimes I fear
I do things
It makes me do things
Do things in real life
That I would not
That I only

ANTHONY
He stops himself
Mid-sentence
Trails off
A shudder passes over him
And he stares out the window
Onto the yellow glow of the Heath
He says to no one in particular

JACK (THE ELDER)
Sometimes when I look onto the Heath
I consider all the ashes
That have been spread upon it

ANTHONY
I have trouble understanding
What he is saying
I cannot focus
I try to keep my eyes open

GEORGE
Anthony
Anthony focus

ANTHONY
He turns suddenly
And begins to prepare the mixture

GEORGE
I don't remember this part
He must have mixed it in the kitchen

JACK (THE ELDER)
One drop
Two drops
Three drops

ANTHONY
His hands shake
As he measures

> GEORGE
> This isn't how it happened for me at all

> JACK (THE ELDER)
> Here

ANTHONY
You first
You seem to need it
More than I do

> JACK (THE ELDER)
> Yes
> The sound

Sound.

ANTHONY
Mine sounds like the ocean crashing
Or a ticking time bomb
And yours?

> JACK (THE ELDER)
> A single wailing voice

Beat.

ANTHONY
Oh
I'm
I'm so sorry
That's a particularly awful one

I suddenly feel quite sorry for him

> JACK (THE ELDER)
> Cheers

JACK *drinks the mixture.*

ANTHONY
It is as he is stretching
His neck back
That I see it

> GEORGE
> My necklace Anthony
> The eye
> To ward off evil

> JACK (THE ELDER)
> That's better

ANTHONY
I am caught by surprise
I consider reaching out
Snatching it
But my arms
They are too like cartilage

Your necklace

> GEORGE
> *My* necklace

ANTHONY
For the second time
He blanches
He quickly recovers

The eye

> JACK (THE ELDER)
> The eye of Horace
> To ward off evil
> An ancient symbol

ANTHONY
Where did you get it?

> GEORGE
> My mother gave it to me

> JACK (THE ELDER)
> Your turn

ANTHONY
I'm fine
Really

> JACK (THE ELDER)
> Wouldn't you like some?

ANTHONY
I'm not due
For another half-hour

> JACK (THE ELDER)
> But the sound

Sound.

ANTHONY
What about it?

> JACK (THE ELDER)
> Don't you hear it?
> It's everywhere
> I'll fix you some

ANTHONY
I realise
I have little choice in the matter
I ask him again
As he prepares

The necklace
Where did you get it?

> JACK (THE ELDER)
> One drop
> Two drops
> Three drops
> A boy

> GEORGE
> Me

ANTHONY
Yes?

> JACK (THE ELDER)
> He gave it to me

> GEORGE
> He didn't give it to me
> He took it

> JACK (THE ELDER)
> Here

ANTHONY
Make mine stronger

> JACK (THE ELDER)
> Are you sure?

> GEORGE
> What are you doing Anthony?

ANTHONY
Yes
Very strong

> JACK (THE ELDER)
> Four drops
> Five

ANTHONY
And did you two
Have a good time?

I can see my question grates
But I can also tell
That the mixture he drank
Is starting to have an effect
He is becoming a live wire
I try to stay focused
Try to stay in control

Did you?

> JACK (THE ELDER)
> Yes

ANTHONY
Stronger

> JACK (THE ELDER)
> Six drops
> Seven

ANTHONY
What did you do?

> JACK (THE ELDER)
> We

GEORGE
It's coming back to me
We met online
He asked

JACK (THE ELDER)
I asked if he wanted to come over
I said we'd have a good time

GEORGE
I asked how much he could pay

JACK (THE ELDER)
I told him I would pay five hundred pounds

GEORGE
Rent was due

JACK (THE ELDER)
He let me

ANTHONY
He let you what?
You can add more
By the way

JACK (THE ELDER)
Are you sure?

GEORGE
Anthony
Be careful

ANTHONY
I've been using for

JACK (THE ELDER)
How long?

ANTHONY
Ten years

JACK (THE ELDER)
Eight
Nine

ANTHONY
You were saying
What he let you do

> GEORGE
> I didn't let him
> He handed me

> JACK (THE ELDER)
> My problem has always been that
> I can hear other people's sounds
> The chems made me realise
> There was a way
> A way to make my sound go quiet
> And theirs too

ANTHONY
I take it you
Put him under

> GEORGE
> The wine Anthony

> JACK (THE ELDER)
> Twelve
> Thirteen
> Fourteen

ANTHONY
And then
And then what did you do?

The question hangs in the air
Like a body from a noose

> JACK (THE ELDER)
> Here

ANTHONY
He holds out the glass

> JACK (THE ELDER)
> Drink

ANTHONY
Though my arm feels detached from my torso
I take the glass from him

The mixture is highly concentrated
I raise it to my lips
(What I hope are my lips)
And stare into his eyes

They are like
Looking into a mirror
Or the future

>   GEORGE
>   Anthony
>   Anthony what are you doing?
>   If you drink that
>   You'll die

ANTHONY
It is a curious property
Of gamma-Butyrolactone
That in its undiluted
Or highly concentrated form
It will melt through plastic
Human skin
However
Is remarkably unaffected
The only sensitive areas
Are the throat
Where it causes a burning sensation
And the
Eyes
Where it causes severe pain

In one movement, ANTHONY *splashes the contents of the glass into* JACK's *eyes.*

>   JACK (THE ELDER)
>   Shit shit shit shit shit

JACK *writhes in pain.*

ANTHONY – *rather clumsily – picks up the bottle.*

ANTHONY *holds the bottle to* JACK's *lips.*

ANTHONY
Jack
Jack Jack Jack

Oh I'm so sorry
How clumsy of me
Here
This will help
This will help

ANTHONY *pours the contents of the bottle down* JACK's *throat.*

JACK *chokes.*

JACK *writhes.*

GEORGE *and* ANTHONY *watch* JACK.

After a moment, JACK *is silent.*

ANTHONY *bends down over* JACK's *body.*

ANTHONY *removes the necklace from* JACK's *neck.*

ANTHONY *searches through* JACK's *pockets.*

He finds the tie clip.

> GEORGE
> Should you call an ambulance?

ANTHONY
He's ingested too much
There's nothing they can do

> GEORGE
> The police?

ANTHONY
They'll treat it as an overdose

> GEORGE
> Even though it's burned his eyes?

ANTHONY
Accidents happen

> GEORGE
> What if they search for fingerprints?
> DNA?

ANTHONY
Then they'll find the other Jack's
The one whose body is lying on the tumulus
The *Ham and High* will report it
As a tragic double overdose

GEORGE
I suppose you're right

ANTHONY *holds out the necklace*.

ANTHONY
Here you are
Your necklace
And Jack's tie clip
Everything is now in order

GEORGE
Thank you for finding them

ANTHONY
Now it's time
For your part of the bargain
You promised to make it
Go away

GEORGE *stares at* ANTHONY.

Sound.

Forever

Sound.

Aren't you going to take it?

Sound.

GEORGE *turns*.

GEORGE
You can keep them

Sound.

GEORGE *walks*.

ANTHONY
George

Sound.

George you promised

Sound.

You promised

Sound.

We shared something

Sound.

We shared

Sound.

We

The sound becomes like the ocean crashing.

Like a time bomb exploding.

Like metal being dragged across asphalt.

Like wailing.

The sound grows and grows.

The sound is deafening.

Blackout.

GLITTER PUNCH

Lucy Burke

Glitter Punch was first performed at Theatre N16, Balham, and The Lion and Unicorn, Kentish Town, with Molly played by Hannah Lawrence and John played by Hadley Smith, and at the King's Head Theatre, Islington, with Molly played by Charlotte Salkind.

The production was revived at the Edinburgh Festival Fringe, August 2017, at Assembly George Square Studios, and transferred to VAULT Festival, London, on 28 February 2018, with the following cast:

MOLLY DAVIES   Emily Stott
JOHN ANDERSON   Anthony Fagan

Director   Peter Taylor
Technician   Rose Hockaday
Producer   Some Riot Theatre

Characters

MOLLY DAVIES, *sixteen*
JOHN ANDERSON, *twenty-seven*

The following action takes place in 2016, over the course of
four months in Salford, Greater Manchester.

Note on Text

A lack of punctuation at the end of a line indicates the next line
should follow on at a pace.

MOLLY, *sixteen, stands centre stage with two Aldi carrier bags full of her belongings.*

MOLLY. This diary belongs to Molly Shannon Davies
Age sixteen
07867374952
mollybaby_2000@btinternet.com
snapchat mollybaby.2000
insta mollybaby.2000

If found return to 39A Welford Street, Salford, England

And do not, I repeat do not, fucking read.

...

MOLLY. It's my first day at college. I'm in the smoking area, there's a chill in the air because it might only be the beginning of September but it's the north of England so let's face it there's always a fucking chill.

JOHN. You got a light?

MOLLY. Some lad with a shitty rolly in his mouth is staring at my freshly lit cigarette and my lighter and I think, that's a stupid question because I obviously do. I hand him the lighter and don't say owt because it's only eight forty-five and I ain't gonna interact with anyone before midday voluntarily.

JOHN. Thanks

MOLLY. He looks how I feel, which is tired and like he wants to be anywhere else but here. Here being college, here being Salford, here being awake at 8.45 a.m. I inhale and the smoke warms my insides and my vision clears a bit and I have this feeling that I want to look at the guy again. There's this look in his eye that tells me he's even further away from being here than I am and I look at his shoes and they're all fancy like actual shoe-shoes and not Reebok Classics like mine. And it might be early but I'm half a cigarette into the day and fuck me he's all handsome and frowny and even though he must be a mentalist to think it's okay to wear proper shoes in this area, I still think we might get on and I want to tell him that. But I'm nowt special like, I'm just Molly and I'm shit with words and that and my tits are too small so I just say

Alright

JOHN. Good morning

MOLLY. Now I'm no Sherlock but what with that voice and those shoes it's pretty clear that this kid definitely isn't from Salford. So I say

Good morning

In a voice like his all posh like. And he says

Nothing.

Rude.

And I think back to what Mum said about how chuffed she is that I'm the first of the Davies family to get into college and how proud she was this morning and that, proper glowing like one of those pictures of Mary in the RE books at primary and I love Mum, I do even though she's a bit of a shit sometimes but well I'm a bit of a shit sometimes cos well we're human int we. And I think about how she made me do some gay-arse pinky promise to give college a go and make friends and that and I look at the kid again and I feel something deep inside me that's like, like preventing me from not looking at him and I say again

Good morning

This time in my own voice like and then well I'm getting a bit pissed off now cos he's still being a rude fuck and I've finished my cigarette and it's cold and I want to go in and I remember it's eight forty-five which is too early when

JOHN. John.

MOLLY. Molly. What form are you?

JOHN. B15, I'm –

MOLLY. Me too!

JOHN. Smoking's bad for you you know?

MOLLY. Loads of things are bad for you. Where you from?

JOHN. London. Place called Chiswick

MOLLY. Then why you in the arse-end of Manchester now?

JOHN. That's a long story

MOLLY. Condense it to ten minutes and I'm interested

JOHN. Fuck it. My dad passed away. Start of this year. I went into a bit of a. I wasn't very well for a while. Had to get away. Was looking for... Moved... Ended up here

MOLLY. Sorry. About your dad and that. And that you ended up here

JOHN. It's alright. It's not your fault

MOLLY. My dad fucked off two years ago. He's not dead like. Just not. Here I guess. He ain't around

JOHN. Sorry

MOLLY. Not your fault. Life innit. I'm going in, I'm cold. See you

JOHN. Oh. Maybe I can borrow your lighter tomorrow?

MOLLY. Maybe.

And I go in and I think, well that was fucking odd.

But my heart is doing this thing where it feels like it's way too big for my chest and it's thumping so hard I think it might actually shoot up my throat, fall right out of my mouth, land at my feet and melt into mush on the ground and all I'll be able to do is watch it just like I'm watching this kid John now, out the window, taking a drag and inhaling deeply as if the weight of the world is on his shoulders and it's all he can do to keep smoking, keep breathing in and out. In and out. In and out.

...

MOLLY. I'm making a habit of getting to college fifteen minutes early every day which is a miracle for me cos I love sleep and I hate people. Usually. I used to crave my first cig of the day but this weird thing's happened where I feel like I'm actually just craving this time with John and the cigarette's just collateral.

JOHN. How was your weekend?

MOLLY. Quiet. Usual.

It wasn't, I had a blazing row with Mum and slept in the bus shelter Saturday night but I int gonna tell him that.

How was yours? Your weekend?

JOHN. I went to see my dad

MOLLY. The dead one?

JOHN. Yeah. The dead one

MOLLY. How was that?

JOHN. Well it was nice to have someone to talk to –

MOLLY. Fuck off John I talk to you every day

JOHN. Was nice to have someone to talk to who didn't interrupt every bloody second

MOLLY. Every bloody second.

Can I. Can I come over? To your house? I'll er, I'll bring you some cigs if you want. Proper ones so you don't have to roll

JOHN. I like to have something to do with my hands. That's why I roll

MOLLY. And he doesn't answer my question and I think that's it, I've fucked it

JOHN. Why don't you come tonight?

MOLLY. And I want to scream and jump about and that and use up all the adrenalin that's rushing through my veins, all this energy I've never ever had before, not on my sixteenth birthday when Dad visited for a surprise and not when my little brother was born. Nowt. And I've never felt an excitement like this before, like a feeling that for once something amazing could happen. But I'm just Molly and I'm shit with words and that and my tits are too small, so I just say

Cool.

And we've decided. And we ain't going back.

...

MOLLY. What's your favourite colour?

JOHN. My favourite –

MOLLY. Colour. Yeah. Sorry, shit question –

JOHN. Green

MOLLY. Right.

JOHN. Yours?

MOLLY. It's a shit –

JOHN. Hmm?

MOLLY. Shit question really. Pink.

JOHN. Right

MOLLY. I have this urge to know every single possible thing about him. Everything. The magnificent and cool stuff. And the shit and boring stuff. I ask him what he had for dinner last night and how many cigarettes he smoked today and whether he had a bath or a shower this morning – cos turns out he's got a bath and a shower in his place which is mental and brilliant and the main reason why I'm always over at his place.

I want to know everything that's happened to him. Was he popular back in London and does he like Twiglets and who's his favourite *Friends* character? And – No, yes and Ross. By the way. And it's like it's not enough to just know all this shit. I want to learn it, to learn him, to learn his face and his smiles and the way he breathes when he's scared but trying not to be. I want to learn what makes him tick and how to make him happy – which is hard, by the way, cos it's hard enough making yourself happy, especially when you're from a place like Salford, let alone making another human happy. But with him, I want to. I want to get it right, I want to learn him perfectly.

I don't think I've ever wanted to learn before. At parents' evening the teachers would tell Mum I needed to 'apply myself more if I wanted to succeed', apart from last parents' evening where Mum turned up late because her knobby boyfriend Knobby-Steve was meant to watch the baby but he'd gone down the pub so she came with the baby but he threw up down us and we had to leave during the headteacher's speech.

But John, he makes me want to learn and that. Want to learn to be better.

...

MOLLY. I go over every Wednesday and Friday. He finishes earlier than me so he waits for me in Sainsbury's car park and he drives us back cos he's got a licence and a car which is mint even if it is a bit messy and has too many empty coffee cups in there. Turns out his house is in the nice bit of Salford, the Quays bit which explains the shoes and the voice and why I never invite him to mine. We're driving back and he pulls into an alleyway, a proper pretty one like, for Salford I mean and I think maybe there's something wrong with the car but it's not the car it's

JOHN *kisses* MOLLY.

And he's kissing me, right on the mouth. And I was getting doubtful that the perfect kiss ever existed, like the ones that Lindsay Lohan used to have in films before she went crazy or on *Don't Tell the Bride* and that. I've kissed two boys before John. One was my cousin when I was four and one was with this lad Burger in Year 8 and both of them were wet and tasted a lot like yogurt which was gross. But when John kisses me it's different. It's like time stops for a bit and I can't hear the traffic out the window and I can't remember what day it is and my head gets all spinny but in a good way like I'm on the waltzers which is my favourite ever ride and not the bad way like when I nicked Mum's vodka and fell down the stairs and was sick afterwards.

He stops kissing me and I feel this ridiculous smile spreading across my face and it's so big I feel like I'm gonna run out of space on my head but I can't help it and it won't stop and he's doing the same anyway so I feel mildly less fucking idiotic.

He's putting his hand on my thigh and it's going higher and higher and then it's not touching my thigh it's touching my knickers and I like it but all I can think is that I wish I would have worn nicer knickers, except it's Friday which is washing day so I only had the shit ones clean. I get this feeling like a bit leaky and that and I can feel myself going bright red because I think I must have come on my period or something, either that or I've pissed myself a bit and I don't know what's worse but they're both equally as bad and I'm panicking and I've fucked it and

JOHN. Should I stop?

MOLLY. Sorry. Yeah. No. I think –

JOHN. It feels like you like it?

MOLLY. I think I've come on maybe, I'm early but. Fuck. Fuck

I'm putting my seatbelt on as if that'll help anything and

JOHN. Shit

MOLLY. I know. I'm sorry I er –

JOHN. Babe you're aroused. You're just. You're not. You've not. You're wet Molly.

MOLLY. And I'm so relieved that I've not pissed myself but John's doing his frowning again which I haven't seen him do in ages

JOHN. You've not done this before have you?

MOLLY. Loads of times.

No.

When you're a virgin and you're sixteen and you're from Salford it's fucking embarrassing. It's like this massive thing that you've got to try and hide only it's not a thing it's like a 'not-thing' which is even trickier to hide, like how do you hide a 'not-thing'? It's like a hole in your life and you can work around it but there's no covering it up because there's nothing to cover. You feel like there's probably definitely something wrong with you which obviously there is I mean my tits are too small and I hate people so I don't know in what world I could have had sex before but I still feel, embarrassed. And different. Like the only sober person at a party or something when everyone else is smashed.

And I don't get why they say you 'lose' your virginity. Because you're not losing anything are you. Are you? You're gaining fucking normality that's how I see it. It's easy to lose something, lost my phone twice in one day last week, always lose my homework, pretty sure I lost my mind the day Dad left but losing my virginity? Not easy mate. Surely it's more about finding something? Finding someone. Who wants you, and who you want. And I think it's John. I do. And I want to tell him this but I'm just Molly and I'm shit with words and that and my tits are too small so I just whisper

Sorry.

And he's kissing me and touching my knickers again and he says

JOHN. Fuck

MOLLY. And it hurts a bit at first. But after that it's not so bad and anyway I love kissing him and he's mine and I'm his and we're safe.

...

MOLLY. I'm in his room. We're on the bed and he's smoking out the window that's next to the bed on his side. It's freezing cos it's November now but he's got his arm wrapped around me and I'm wearing his jumper which makes me feel ace and I can smell him on me even after I take the jumper off, like he's marked me but in a good way like a love bite and not in a bad way like a cat pissing on a tree or a tramp stamp or chlamydia.

I'm wondering how that cigarette feels, with his lips wrapped around it and then I know I've gone loopy because I'm wishing I could be an inanimate object and I'm looking at the cig and I'm looking at his mouth and it's proper, it's like beautiful. And his front tooth's a bit crooked. And the smoke's hypnotic and we're breathing in and out. In and out. In and out.

There's pills next to his bed cos he's says he used to take happy pills but he hasn't needed them since he met me which makes me feel a bit confused but mainly all rosy inside and only a little bit sad that someone as cool as him ever had to take happy pills to begin with.

Why did you take 'em? The pills and that?

JOHN. I –

MOLLY. Because loads of sad stuff was happening?

JOHN. Erm. The opposite, I guess.

MOLLY. You what?

JOHN. Sad stuff was happening, yeah. Quite a lot. Like my dad
and stuff. But I actually took them before all the crap with my
dad. When things were happy, well when they were supposed
to be, you know? Lots of amazing stuff was happening and
I felt, erm nothing. A bit, very empty you know?

That probably doesn't make sense.

MOLLY. It makes sense. And I'm thinking how maybe I've
missed a trick because that's been the story of my fucking life
and I ain't never had any happy pills helping me along. And
I wonder what they taste like and if, just for a second, maybe
I could try one and see what happens and be all buzzy and
awake feeling and I wonder if they're as delicious as Calpol.

When my brother come out, of my mum like. I was in the
room and that cos well, Knobby-Steve was meant to be the
birthing partner but he'd got too pissed the night before and
not come home and I love Mum, I do, even though she gives
Knobby-Steve too many chances but like, I do love her so
I went with her to the hospital and I was in the room when
she pushed him out and that. I stood at like, the vag end
where he actually come out and I saw the blood and the gore
and the shit and the waters cos he came out in the waters like
what I did which is quite rare and that and is meant to be a
lucky sign although I've never felt lucky or owt.

There was so much noise, just sound after sound of machines
and doctors and Mum swearing blue murder and swearing at
me as if it was my fault she was pushing a watermelon out of
her insides and it was loud and I hate loud things because it
reminds me too much of being at home and the block of flats
and the Manchunian Way but when he come out, his head
came first and that and – it just went quiet. – Well it wasn't
really quiet, Mum was still swearing and the doctor was
telling her to push and the machines were beeping in the way
that they should be beeping but to me it was. Well it was
magic. Literally magic like how can something so pure come
out of such a chaotic fucking situation? And how can he

belong to us now? And to Mum and Knobby-Steve.
Although I tried really, really hard not to think about him
belonging to Knobby-Steve.

And I think this was one of those moments that John was
talking about where I was supposed to feel like, I don't know,
overjoyed and that? Happy like. But all I could feel. My main
feeling, I was jealous. Jealous of this new human that hadn't
fucked up or been fucked up and had every chance to turn out
amazing. How can you feel jealous of a little baby? How can
you feel jealous of anything Knobby-Steve had a hand in
creating? But, I was like. I wanted to start again. To have a
chance at not being sad. Of growing up, happy.

The baby cries all the time anyway. And his first word was
was fuck, last week actually, so he definitely ain't so pure
any more. Maybe one day he'll watch Mum push out her
next kid with her next guy and maybe he'll feel just as
jealous as what I did, and then guilty for feeling jealous, and
then relieved that the new kid turns out equally fucked, and
then even more guilty for feeling that.

Or maybe he'll meet someone, like how I've met John, and
realise that even though we're in Salford and even though
Mum's our mum and Knobby-Steve's, well, there, there's still
a chance that you can feel happy in the moments you're meant
to feel happy. And not jealous or empty or guilty. Just happy.
And I realise that I definitely do not for a second want to try
John's happy pills, and I don't want him to have them ever
again either. But I do understand, why, like he wanted them
and that. And I want to tell him all this but I'm just Molly and
I'm shit with words and my tits are too small so I just say

Yeah.

John tells me about his dad and what a legend he was

JOHN. Heart attack got him in the end. Fifty-six years old.
Too soon

MOLLY. He tells me the grief counsellor gave him this book that
said 'When someone dies, it feels like the hole in your gum
when a tooth falls out. You can chew, you can eat, you have
plenty of other teeth, but your tongue keeps going back to that
empty place, where all the nerves are still a little raw.' I wrote
it down like, cos I thought it was quite nice and that but

JOHN. It's all bollocks

MOLLY. Cos I guess it's not a tooth-shaped hole at all

JOHN. It's a bloody cavern

MOLLY. And I want to fix it, to mend the hole, the cavern
whatever that is when it's at home but I don't know how. And
I don't want to look at him any more because I can see too
much and it's hurting my insides and then there's this big fat
tear rolling down his cheek and sploshing onto the bed and
I've never seen a man cry before and I've never seen John cry
before but fuck me I want to make it stop. I want to tell him
that I think maybe, the hole probably won't heal, probably
ever. Cos it's life and it's shit sometimes, a lot of the time. But
maybe he might get used to the hole and he can eat around it
and still enjoy stuff like crisps and cigarettes and that. Because
that's what happened to me after Dad left. And I want to tell
him that he's fixed a whole load of gaping caverns in my life
that I didn't even know were there and I think, I hope maybe,
I can do that for him too. But I'm just Molly and I'm shit with
words and that so I just squeeze his hand and he squeezes back
and it hurts my hand cos he's squeezing so tight as if if he let
go he'd fall over or die or do a bit more crying which I don't
want, so I just let him keep squeezing and he's making these
noises like inside his body that I think if he let them out might
be loud but they're coming from inside which is even sadder
and then he stops making the noises and doing the crying and

JOHN. I think I'm falling in love with you

MOLLY. And I say

Fuck off

Because that's mad that, cos no one's ever been in love with
me. No one's ever even fancied me, apart from Burger in Year
8 but that doesn't count because I don't think anything counts
coming from a lad who voluntarily calls himself Burger. And
besides, he can't love me, because I'm just Molly aren't I and
I'm shit with words and my tits are too small. But

JOHN. Molly. I love you

MOLLY. And he says it looking deep into the pit of my
stomach. Well obviously he isn't looking at my stomach
because that'd be weird wouldn't it, he's looking, staring into

my eyes but I can feel it in my stomach, right in the gut like someone's punched me too hard but a nice punch like, a glittery punch or something. And I love him. Course I do. I love him. And all at once it's like everything in the world makes sense. All the shit stuff and the average stuff and just the stuff-stuff, it makes sense and I want to tell him that. And I want him to be like my forever person and I want him to keep punching me with his glitter punch and never stop and to keep looking at me in that way that he's looking at me now in a way that sees and not just looks and I want to tell him that. But I just say

Me too

Because I'm just Molly aren't I and I'm shit with words. And my tits are still too small.

...

MOLLY. I used to think I'd experienced everything there ever was to experience ever. Which when you're only sixteen and three quarters, is pretty fucking scary. All the fun stuff, all the stuff you're meant to wait to do, I've done it mate. And I'm not showing off like, or if I am then only a little bit but if I'm honest I'm glad I didn't wait because I think it might just have made them all the more disappointing which would have made me dead sad and that. More sad even.

I went to this party last year, at The Horse and Jockey where my mum works, I had to go cos at that point we were living out of Knobby-Steve's car and so it was either the party with Mum or the car with Knobby-Steve and even though The Horse and Jockey is a bit too loud and smells like Mini Cheddars it's better than an evening chain smoking with Knobby-Steve who can barely string a sentence together and swears too fucking much and voted for Brexit.

Everyone at the party seemed to be having way more fun than me, which isn't unusual, but like they were dead smiley and their eyes were all blinky and wide and I ain't never seen people that happy especially in Salford in winter in The Horse and Jockey. There were like more people in the toilets than out at the bar which I thought was weird because why would people be peeing so much? And why would the peeing last so long? And there was all this laughing like coming from inside the toilets, which I thought was odd because last time I checked, going toilet isn't that funny it's pretty boring and is just an excuse to check my Instagram which is never funny just boring and filled with too many filters. I thought maybe they might be doing something other than peeing, like gossiping or smoking or doing blowjobs, but whatever it was I hadn't had a laugh in ages. And I wanted to. So I went in.

I was right. Because they weren't peeing, the cubicles were all free and that, only they weren't gossiping or smoking or giving head either. All by the sink there was this white powder, loads of it like. This woman with a rolled-up fiver was leaning over and proper hoovering it up the fiver and into her nose and blinking and laughing and I wanted to run into the cubicle and lock the door and stay in there for a really long time because I might not be the sharpest tool but I knew that none of this shit was legal. And it wasn't even like the fun kind of illegal like bunking off school or... skinny-dipping, it was proper, throw-you-in-jail, tell-your-mum-on-you illegal. And I wanted to run. Only I wanted to laugh too, and have fun and for fucking once be a part of something rather than standing on the edges.

The woman gives me the fiver and tells me that she doesn't usually share but that I'm Mandy's daughter and Mandy let them bring it in so she'd make an exception. And I did it and I pretended it was Sherbet Dib Dab and it was fine and my face kind of felt like it was eating itself and the next day I was really really sad.

That's it.

I didn't like it. I didn't like drinking and I didn't like that and I didn't like smoking at first but it grew on me. And I didn't know that there was much else to try. I have been happy, like when I was younger and that, like the time the tooth fairy left me two quid instead of one. And I've been sad, like countless times. I've been embarrassed like whenever I have to go anywhere with Knobby-Steve. And I've been scared, like, whenever I have to go anywhere with Knobby-Steve.

I kind of thought that was it.

But when John tells me he loves me and I say it back, I know there's more and it's like, like someone's opened the curtains and this fucking magnificent, sunshiney view comes streaming in and I didn't even know it was there. I didn't think sunshiney views ever even existed in Salford only they do cos I'm looking at one, and feeling the heat of the sun on my skin and it's all mine to reach out and touch and it's John and he's here and I feel, excited.

...

MOLLY. We're going to Llandudno for the weekend

JOHN. Just me and you

MOLLY. He's inherited a place from his dad, some holiday home

JOHN. Probably a bloody mess

MOLLY. But good enough for us

JOHN. Good enough for us.

MOLLY. John wakes me up proper early, like stupid o'clock early. And I'm a grumpy fuck, for a second until I remember that I love him and we're on holiday and he could wake me up at whatever hour of the day and still make me ridiculously happy.

JOHN. Come on

MOLLY. Where are we going?

JOHN. You'll see

MOLLY. And I'm throwing on my clothes and his hoodie and my trainers and he's grabbing me by the hand and pulling me out the door as if where ever it is that we're going isn't gonna last for much longer so we have to get there pronto.

We're on the beach. It's pitch black. And even though it's John and I love him and his crooked front tooth is fucking beautiful, it's still pitch fucking black and so I'm starting to slightly resent being dragged out of bed and out of his arms and into the cold.

What the fuck John?

JOHN. Wait for it

MOLLY. Wait for what? I'm going back to bed

JOHN. Molly. Molly! Have a bit of bloody patience will you?

MOLLY. What are we doing here? I don't like it. I'm freezing

JOHN. Why don't you just wait? For a second Molly. Where are you... You can never bloody wait for one second

MOLLY. It's creepy as fuck, fucking fuck this

JOHN. Jesus Christ Molly you're acting like such a... Come back will you?

MOLLY. And I'm walking away, and I'm pissed off. Cos I'm tired and cold and I want to be cuddling and not stood in the middle of fucking nowhere looking at the middle of fucking nothing. And I'm trying to get back to the house and I can't see where I'm going and I trip and a whole bunch of sand scuffs upwards and flies into my face and

JOHN. Good things come to those who wait Moll.

MOLLY. And I turn back around. And it's not dark any more. It's getting lighter. And I can see John sprawled on the sand and the sun's rising over him and lighting him up and it's the prettiest picture I've ever seen only it's not a picture it's real life and it's my life and I thought perfection didn't exist, couldn't ever exist except I've found it and it's here and it's John and it's mine.

Well and then I'm embarrassed. Cos I just threw a right strop and I want to go sit by John and squeeze him and hold his hand and watch the sun rise with him only I'm embarrassed and I've fucked it cos he's seen the real me, the ugliness and the impatience and the fucking child and

JOHN. Sit with me

MOLLY. And I do. And it's the best day of my life.

I've never seen real sand before. Sand that's not in a sandpit like. And I've definitely never seen the sea before. Only on TV like, and on the postcards Dad sends me every blue moon which I'm pretty sure are fake because Dad was always scared-as of flying and besides they always come with a Manchester postal stamp.

The sun's risen now, so all I'm looking at is the sea and the sand and John and this bright-blue fairy-fucking-tale sky and it makes me feel dead small. Like wondering how many other people are looking at the same sky and the same sea and feeling just as small as what I am. And for the first time in my life I actually feel lucky, lucky to be alive and here and breathing and that. And not disabled or starving or like those little black kids they show you in adverts to make you give fifty pee a month.

And I want to be in this moment for ever, only I know I can't cos time will go on and the sun will go down again and I'll have to go back to Salford, back to Mum and Knobby-Steve and my brother and our too-small flat and the smoke and the arguing and the baby's constant fucking crying. And I'm scared to go back but I'm not. I'm scared because I might not get to have another picture-perfect, smacked-in-the-gut, happy-as-fuck moment, but I'm not scared because wherever I go, I'm with John now and he's coming too and we're an us and it's mint and there ain't nothing can break us apart.

...

MOLLY. We're driving back. To Salford. And I think John might have just actually definitely read my mind cos he says

JOHN. It doesn't matter where we are as long as I'm with you Moll.

MOLLY. He's started calling me Moll which usually I hate like if my mum or anyone else does it or owt. But I like it when he says it because let's be honest I love him so he could say anything he wanted or fart the alphabet and I'd still think he was the bee's knees. Cos love does that to you turns out. Makes you all strange in the head but good strange like one of those cats on the internet that can play the piano and not bad strange like dairy-free milk or *Takeshi's Castle* or Donald Trump.

I've packed the snacks and he's made a playlist on Spotify. He's named the playlist

JOHN. John and Moll's Mix Tape

MOLLY. Which he thinks is hilarious and really cute and that but I don't get because what the fuck's a mix tape when it's at home? The songs are a bit old and that so I can't join in the singing but that's fine cos I'm a shit singer anyway so

I just sit there and hold his hand while he sings and drives and eats crisps and it's fucking marvellous.

I haven't told my mum where I've been all weekend cos well, she hasn't asked and she never does. She's had to take on more shifts at The Horse and Jockey and she has to stay even later on the weekends and she does her best but let's be honest it's a bit shit because I never ever see her any more since Dad left. Her boyfriend, Knobby-Steve is a right knob and makes our house smell like cigarettes because he smokes inside so I had to nick Mum's perfume to try and cover the cig smell that hangs around my clothes, her proper nice perfume too CK Into You that Dad bought her before he left and I think John notices because

JOHN. You smell perfect

MOLLY. And I try not to think about the fact that I don't smell perfect at all, I smell like Knobby-Steve's cigarettes covered up by Mum's perfume which Dad probably got knock-off because let's face it we're not the kind of people that can afford CK Into You, and then that got me feeling bad for nicking Mum's only one nice thing that Dad ever gave her and that makes me even angrier with Knobby-Steve the dosser who never buys us owt nice because he won't get his arse down the Jobcentre so he's always skint. But then

JOHN. It's just me and you Moll. Me and you against the world

MOLLY. And all at once the shit thoughts melt away and all I can see is John and all I can feel is my hand in his and it's like, like, I don't have to rob my mum's perfume any more because John is my very own CK Into You covering up all the shit and making everything perfect. And I want to tell him that but I'm just Molly and I'm shit with words and that. And I'm still hoping John hasn't noticed that my tits are too small so I just say

Yeah.

And eat a Pringle and hold his hand a bit tighter.

...

MOLLY. We're at a junction.

This car's coming towards us and I know it's gonna slow down because it's got to because if it doesn't it's hitting John square-on so it's got to and at first I think the car is slowing down but then I realise it's me that's slowing down cos everything's going into this weird slow motion like what you see in films and on TV and that and this car's got to slow down cos it's got to and I can feel each bead of sweat dripping down my forehead into my eyes and it stings and this car's got to slow down cos it's got to and I can feel John's grip loosening on mine cos he's trying to steady the steering wheel with both hands and I'm trying to keep hold of his hand but I can't and this car's got to slow down because fucking it's got to and I'm waiting for my life to flash in front of my eyes but there's fuck-all apart from me and John and kissing and smoking and eating crisps and fucking and fucking this car's got to slow down cos it's got to and –

The paramedics are here. They're crowding round John and these strangers are crowding round them gawping as if we're the latest episode of *Corrie* and they can do one and I just want to get to John but they're carting him into an ambulance and I'm trying to get through so I can go with him but they won't let me because they're wrapping me in this sheet like a turkey that's about to go in the oven at Christmas and I'm not a turkey I'm just Molly and I want my boyfriend but they're driving him away, and they're asking me for his licence and where we were going and where we've been and who my next of kin is whatever that means when it's at home. And the playlist, the Mix Tape sorry, it's still playing. It's still playing. John and Moll's Mix Tape. Only it's not John and Moll cos John's not here and he's not singing and I don't know the words so I've fucked it. And all I can think of is that playlist. Playing to an empty car. With no one to sing along any more. And I'm as redundant as that playlist now John's not here. Cos there ain't anyone else who knows my words like John. No one to sing along.

...

MOLLY. When I get to the hospital he's all wired up to these machines and there's a tube in his throat and this beeping constant beeping which I think is a good thing because it means he's alive but it doesn't seem like a good thing because nothing about what I'm seeing right now seems like a good thing. It seems pretty fucked if you ask me. And I'd give anything for it to have been me that the car crashed into and the nurse says he's in a coma and they don't know when, or if, he's going to wake up but that I should talk to him anyway and that he might be able to hear me. But I'm just Molly and I'm shit with words and my... –

Hi John. It's me. Sorry, Molly. Your eyes are shut so you don't really know who 'me' is do you. I hope you're okay. I was dead excited to go to Llandudno with you. Shit, not dead excited. Not dead anything. Sorry John. Proper. I was proper excited to go to Llandudno with you. No one's ever taken me away before, not even to Blackpool or owt. So thanks. It was mint. Perfect and that.

I er – I hope you're not in too much pain or anything.

College is shit. Same old. It's raining like every day and I've nowhere to go on Wednesdays and Fridays now except last Friday I accidentally walked across to Sainsbury's car park cos I forgot like but then you weren't there cos you were here and that was a bit sad like. But I didn't cry or owt. I'm not being a pussy or owt.

They're giving me counselling at college, for the 'special circumstances' that I've found myself in. It's bollocks John, they can't talk to me like you do, don't know my words, can't sing along like you do.

I er – I really fucking love you John. I love you. I'd really like you to stay alive yeah? I don't really know what I was doing till I found you. Just coasting I suppose. But then I found you and everything was pretty ace and I woke up proper happy and I smiled a lot, we smiled a lot didn't we John? So you can't go yet, just not yet it's a bit soon you know?

Do you know like, do you know when your dad, went, and they told you to say your goodbyes? I think they want me to do that but 'scuse my French, there's fucking no way. I ain't gonna John because you're not going anywhere right? I know you're not. It's me and you John. Me and you against the world, John and Moll's Mix Tape right?

I haven't got anything else. I'm just gonna hold your hand
for a bit if that's okay? That crash John, it was nothing,
you're way stronger. It was just a fucking glitter punch
okay? Okay? I'm done now.

...

MOLLY. I think my time with John is probably, definitely over.
Because well that nurse, she said he might not wake up and
even though I think he might wake up I'm not as smart as the
nurse so.

When Dad left, I thought he probably, definitely would come
back, and I waited and waited, and I thought he'd definitely
come back but he didn't. And I went to his work and he
wasn't there and I called his phone and a woman picked up.
So I'm starting to think that maybe John probably, definitely
won't come back either. I think, probably all the best people
like Dad and John and that, I think sooner or later they just
fuck off and leave me with Mum and Knobby-Steve and my
brother who won't stop crying these days as if it was him
who'd just lost the love of his life and not me.

And I think I'll always be left with Mum and Steve or Mum
and Ian or Mum and Chris or whoever the fuck she brings
home next. Because my mum, well she seems to only bring
home the proper shit ones these days and I used to think she
was proper dumb and that but then well I thought, maybe
she's realised that the best ones leave and the shit ones stay
so she brings people like Steve and Ian and Chris and that
until she gets bored and she can be the one who fucks off to
find another Steve or Ian or Chris and that. Maybe she's a
fucking genius.

And I think maybe after John, I would do the same, I could,
do the same. I'd bring back a shit one and not a best one
except there's no way. An after-John won't exist, because
after John there's nothing but Mum and Knobby-Steve and
college and Salford just like there was before John and I int
doing that again. No way. There won't be an after-John,
there won't be an after-Molly and there definitely won't be
an after-Molly-and-John, we're going to survive for ever, in
here, in fucking here.

She is referring to her stomach. She tries to recreate the feeling of the 'glitter punch' she experienced when falling in love with John only this time with her own hands. It doesn't work. It is horrible to watch.

Because it's too late and he's in my blood and he's poison but a good poison like cannabis and not a bad poison like cyanide or gone-off chicken, or rohypnol.

MOLLY *'s phone rings.*

Hello?

...

MOLLY. John's in a coma for a month. But he survives. Cos he's a fucking legend. And even when life tries its best to fuck with him he sticks two fingers right back at it. My John. But there's a problem. Cos even after he wakes up when I get to college for our cigarette at eight forty-five he ain't there. And when I go into form class at nine he ain't there. And I knew he wouldn't be, they warned me and that so it wasn't a shock but it still is and everyone's staring at me and they can fuck right off and I think I'm starting to feel a bit like what John must have felt when he was talking about the caverns and that, which I googled by the way and turns out it's a just a hole but bigger. Who'd have thunk it? But I'm feeling this cavern in my mouth and in my belly and in my eyes from where we used to look at each other but now we can't. We've got a new form teacher instead. Because after the accident I suppose it all came out, about me and John and how it's not allowed and that and how he can't teach no more. He can't teach here and he can't teach ever and it's all my fault. Because I tried to fix the holes in his life and I just wound up making even more holes. Cos I'm just Molly, and I'm shit with words and my tits are too small and I should have left it well alone but I didn't.

They told me that

'The sexual offences act of 2003 states a sexual relationship between someone who is in a position of trust and a person to whom that trust extends, is criminal.'

And that even though I'm sixteen, it's still against the law because

'You're vulnerable Molly, and Mr Anderson abused his position of power.'

I'm not vulnerable, I'm not. I'm from Salford I ain't vulnerable mate. And it's bullshit anyway because if I went somewhere else, and this is completely true by the way, if I went to Our Lady's or Hulme Grammar or anywhere else and I was still with John then cos we met out or in Sainsbury's or whatever, then John wouldn't be in this shit. It's purely because I went to his, because he's my, was my… And that doesn't make sense. And I wanted to go to Hulme Grammar but I couldn't get in cos I'm just Molly aren't I and I'm shit with words and that. I'm not clever and I don't know much. I mean I was doing travel and tourism for fuck's sake, I'm not clever. But I know this, John's not being punished for fucking me, he's being punished because of the way the fucking came about. Which is bollocks.

And if anyone is vulnerable then it's him. He's the most gentle man I know, he's not malicious or owt. His dad just died. My dad isn't dead. He's not around but as far as I know he ain't dead and I've never experienced grief like what John told me he went through this year. And when he finally woke up after the accident he said that I was like, like fucking golden light in a pit of darkness that he was trying to climb out of or whatever. And he said that meeting me, fuck knows why, but

JOHN. Meeting you Moll. It's made me better.

MOLLY. And he said sometimes it takes losing someone you love to realise that if you find another kind of love then you've gotta cling on to it and not let go and keep punching it with your glitter punches for ever. And

JOHN *and* MOLLY. Fuck the consequences.

MOLLY. Well now I've lost something that I love. And I'm not allowed to feel his glitter punches again. We're not allowed to see each other no more. The police want me to press charges whatever that means when it's at home, so that his name will go on this list with like rapists and paedos and kiddie-fiddlers and actual bad people not good people like John. Fuck that. There's no way. He's my forever person. And we've got a plan.

MOLLY *picks up the carrier bags from the beginning of the play. Scene is as it was at the start of the play.*

I've got my stuff, I had to pack dead quick while Mum was at work and Knobby-Steve took my only weekend bag last time Mum kicked him out so I had to use the Aldi bags I found in the carrier-bag drawer under the sink. I couldn't fit much stuff in but it's okay because I don't have a lot of stuff anyway and what I do have smells like cigs and John said he'll get me new stuff when we get there.

I've never been on a plane before, I'm proper excited and only a little bit scared but mainly excited because I'll get to see inside the clouds and that and John said all the houses are gonna look dead little and the college and the flat and Knobby-Steve are gonna get smaller and smaller till we don't even have to worry about them ever at all.

John said it's me and him, me and him against the world.

I got Mum's credit card out of the drawer where she keeps all her secret things like her weed and her cigs and her Fruit Pastilles which she never shares, and I took a picture of it like John said and sent it to him so he could book the plane and make all the arrangements and that. John said he needed more because he wants us to stay somewhere dead fancy and that and I don't really have any money but I do have a weekly saver that Dad used to do for me. I know because I've got this bank book with a little picture of a cartoon cat on the front who's waving and I think that's supposed to make me want to like trust the bank and stuff but it could have a picture of a fucking anything on and I wouldn't care so long as my dad was still topping it up like what he said he would. I've got one hundred and thirty-six pounds and eighty-one pee in there and I asked John should I draw it out but he said he would because he's over twenty-five and I'm not so they might get suspicious if I tried to do it.

John said he needed to be doubly, triply, surely sure that no one would find out about our plan and that so I had to promise I wouldn't tell Mum or leave a note or even say bye to the baby or owt. Mum's never in anyway so I probably might not even ever miss her but not saying goodbye to the baby, I think that was the worst bit. Even though he cries all the time and he's not potty-trained and I get in trouble every time he swears, it was still the worst bit like. But I know, I think he'll be okay and that. With Mum. Cos they're family, blood and that's got to mean something, I'm just not sure what...

John said we're family now. And he's a bit late like but I know he's on his way. And he'll pick me up and we'll drive away and fly away till all our worries are as small as the tiny houses we'll see out the window on the plane. And he is a bit late like but I sent him the bank details like what he asked and I feel like I love him so much I want to give him every part of me but that's impossible cos really I'm just a person with arms and legs and small tits and how do you give someone every aspect of your being when it's still, attached? So I just gave him the money and this promise that it's us now, for definite and forever, me and him against the world and when I see him I'll give him my Aldi bags and a kiss and a squeeze and the rest of my life. Our life together.

I'm nervous about travelling like cos I've never travelled before, but then I remember how John left London and moved to Salford and I wonder if he travelled anywhere else before that and I think he must be pretty good at doing travelling now so I know he'll look after me.

I light a cig. And I close my eyes. And it's like he's standing right there, next to me. Breathing in and out, in and out, in and out. And his glitter punches have knocked everything into the right order for the first time in my life ever. And it's beautiful. It's fucking beautiful.

BURKAS AND BACON BUTTIES

Shamia Chalabi & Sarah Henley

Burkas and Bacon Butties was first performed on 14 February 2018, at VAULT Festival, London, with the following cast:

YUSUF	Antony Bunsee
SHAZIA	Shamia Chalabi
JEAN	Holly Joyce
CHRIS	Timothy O'Hara
YASMIN	Lisa Zahra

At the time of going to print the role of Ashraf was still to be cast.

Directors	Sarah Butcher
	& Sarah Henley
Design Consultant	Tom Rogers
Lighting Designer	Alex Lewer
Sound Designer	Jon Everett
Graphic Designer	Alex Lewer
Producer	Tara Finney Productions

Thanks

Burkas and Bacon Butties would not have been possible without the support of:

Arts Council England
The Peggy Ramsay Foundation
Shoreditch Town Hall
Arcola Theatre
ArtsEd

For more information, please visit www.tarafinney.com

Characters

YUSUF
ASHRAF
SHAZIA
JEAN
YASMIN
CHRIS

Scene One

We see an empty cab with the hazard lights on, Arabic music blaring out. There are fragrance trees hanging off the mirror along with some '99 names of Allah' prayer beads. There's a plastic bag with Arabic writing on it on the passenger seat and a few empty mugs littered around the cab. The radio crackles.

YUSUF. Driver 1154, can I have your location?

Pause.

1154, please come in, can I have your location?

Pause.

ASHRAF, COME IN, MAN! We have a job for you!

ASHRAF *rushes back to the car, hands full with coffee, a pie, some Hula Hoops and a cigarette. He spills the coffee on himself as he gets into the car and presses the receiver.*

ASHRAF. Shit! Shit! Yes I'm here!

YUSUF. You can't be taking these liberties! Let me guess, picking up snacks?

ASHRAF. No, no, nothing like that.

YUSUF. Coffee then?

ASHRAF. Excuse me but I am professional – no stopping while working, brother, okay? You still on that diet?

YUSUF. You know Hafifah – she's tap-tap-tap in my head – lose weight, stop smoking, this, that. But *Inshallah* I feel good! You should try it too!

ASHRAF. Yusuf, I have already a wife and a daughter – there is no more space for a nagging-horse brother as well!

A beat.

YUSUF. I saw Shazia in the Grand Arcade the other day. Brother – when's she gonna start –

ASHRAF. I'm working on it.

YUSUF. She was with someone – a man.

ASHRAF. Probably a work colleague.

YUSUF. She was holding his hand.

A beat.

You should talk to her, be strict – get her to –

ASHRAF. I am, I am.

YUSUF. For the family, Ashraf – we can't have this. I won't allow it.

ASHRAF. Oh big 'welcome home, Ashraf', isn't it? 'No snack breaks'… 'watch your daughter'… anything else? Am I breathing too loudly? Want me to iron my underpants some more? As my loving brother, you could be asking me how Egypt was.

Pause.

YUSUF. How was Egypt?

ASHRAF *relaxes into the conversation, putting a single Hula Hoop on each forkful of pie and then adding some of his 'special sauce' from a bottle in the cup holder.*

ASHRAF. Fantastic man, good food, relaxation – no stress.

YUSUF. No stress? I heard about the suicide bombs. Fundamentalist idiots.

ASHRAF. Yes but the protest – it was beautiful. The Christians all joined hands to protect the brothers while we prayed in the square.

YUSUF. And of course Yasmin –

ASHRAF. Finally.

YUSUF. Look – after shift come to the café with us? We go have some tea, talk –

ASHRAF. Sounds good – what time? I'm picking Shazia up.

YUSUF. Shit! This pick-up – I forgot – Café Bruciani's –

ASHRAF. Ah yes!

YUSUF. Mrs… Jean –

ASHRAF. Don't give me nightmares!

YUSUF. Smith.

ASHRAF. الحمد لله. (*Alhamd lilah!*) [Praise be to God!]

> ASHRAF *takes another forkful of pie with a Hula Hoop on it and crunches down.*

YUSUF. You *are* eating!

ASHRAF. Outrageous!

YUSUF. I can see your location. You're at Galloway's?!

ASHRAF. You got me! The best pies in Wigan, spiced it up with some of my special sauce!

YUSUF. Ah, bring me one, brother?

ASHRAF. Sorry… it's impossible.

YUSUF. Why?

ASHRAF. Your wife would kill me.

Scene Two

Later that day. ASHRAF *is waiting in the car, smoking. He's slicking down what little hair he has with a brush, checking his teeth – trying to floss with a taxi receipt. He puts out the cigarette and tries to waft the smoke out. He then sprays some Joop from his bag of duty-free around the car.*

SHAZIA *arrives and takes her engagement ring off, moving it to another finger. She opens the door to get in and* ASHRAF *moves the plastic bag on the seat to his lap.*

ASHRAF. Hello, baby! Just some shells there – sorry. What, no hug?

> *He tries to hug her but she's rigid.*

> Shaz –

SHAZIA. You said you'd be gone a month.

Pause.

I thought something had happened.

ASHRAF. Like what? I got stuck in the pyramids? I became a mummy? Got eaten by a camel?

SHAZIA. Not funny.

Pause.

Didn't you even want to know how I was?

ASHRAF. Baby – it was busy, and...

SHAZIA. Right.

Pause.

I was really worried – those attacks, the news –

ASHRAF. I brought you a present.

He passes her the bag with Arabic writing on.

SHAZIA. You think you can buy forgiveness, is that it? Is it jewellery?

ASHRAF. I'm a taxi driver – not a millionaire!

SHAZIA. Or perfume? I see you bought yourself some Joop. Nuts?!

ASHRAF. Special five-star gold-standard the best of bee's knees Egyptian nuts –

SHAZIA. Wait... that you've clearly opened and started eating!

ASHRAF. I got a bit hungry... it's the thought that counts, *habibi*!

SHAZIA. Thanks.

ASHRAF. In Arabic?

SHAZIA. *Shukraan.*

ASHRAF turns the radio on. Whitney Houston, 'I Wanna Dance with Somebody' plays. ASHRAF sings and SHAZIA joins in. The radio starts to crackle and YUSUF's *voice can be heard talking to another driver.* ASHRAF *switches the taxi radio off and turns Whitney down.*

Dad... I need to tell you something and –

ASHRAF. Yusuf saw you the other day.

SHAZIA. Where? I didn't see him – why didn't he say hi?

ASHRAF. In the Grand Arcade... he said you were with a man – holding hands.

SHAZIA. Oh.

Silence.

ASHRAF. Have you thought about the headscarf thing? Please. For me, *habibi*.

ASHRAF *fumbles around in his door and pulls out a piece of paper, he hands it to* SHAZIA.

SHAZIA (*reading*). Spicy-sauce name ideas: 'Sauce and Spice and All Things Nice', 'Kiss My Sauce', 'Wigan Spice', 'Ashraf's Special Sauce'.

ASHRAF. It's good innit?

SHAZIA. You definitely can't use the last one.

ASHRAF. Why? It does what it says on the tin? If Captain Birdseye can sell his fishy fingers then I can have my special sauce.

SHAZIA. Fish fingers.

ASHRAF. I've been working on some new flavours, and its 'mwaah'. I'm going to speak to Tony at the market... Mr Nando had to start somewhere innit?

SHAZIA. Yep!

They listen to the radio for a few beats.

ASHRAF. So you'll think about the headscarf thing though, yes?

She reaches into the plastic bag to get some nuts.

SHAZIA. How's quitting smoking going?

ASHRAF. Good. I'm feeling good. *Inshallah.*

SHAZIA. So what's this?

She presents a pack of duty-free cigarettes to him.

Spraying Joop everywhere doesn't mean I can't smell it.

ASHRAF *takes the cigarettes off her and leans across to put them in the glovebox. As he opens it a pack of pictures falls out and* SHAZIA *picks them up.*

ASHRAF. Leave them. I'll get them!

SHAZIA *looks through the pictures.*

SHAZIA. What? This is a... you're married?

ASHRAF. No, no, I'm not. I'm... engaged! This is a typical Egyptian engagement.

SHAZIA. Barely worth mentioning.

ASHRAF. Don't be sarcastic.

SHAZIA. How do you want me to be?

ASHRAF. Happy? Or silent.

Silence.

Look – I didn't go there to get... engaged, but it was your Uncle Abdelal. He kept on saying I needed someone to take care of me, being divorced was no good. I didn't really want to but he introduced me, made me go along and –

SHAZIA. And forced you to get engaged? Yeah, I mean you look miserable, so unhappy... poor thing!

SHAZIA *picks up a picture and looks closely.*

I mean, her dress, all the guests – you're married, aren't you.

ASHRAF. Yes.

SHAZIA. You didn't think to invite me.

There's a moment of quiet.

ASHRAF. I'm lonely. You're busy – you have your own life, your boyfriend – which I could say a lot more about but... it's just me here. I get back from work and it's just me. I wake up all alone. I spend the day with strangers. I need somebody... to talk about the day with. And she's nice. She's got a good heart –

SHAZIA. Pretty.

ASHRAF. Yes but more than that – we laugh.

SHAZIA. How old is she?

ASHRAF. My age.

SHAZIA. Dad?!

ASHRAF. Okay... a bit younger.

SHAZIA. DAD?!

ASHRAF. Okay, okay, she's thirty-nine.

SHAZIA. Is she coming here?

ASHRAF. Soon. She's applying for the papers.

SHAZIA. You're her ticket.

ASHRAF. She's not like that – she's educated, a professor in a school. She's willing to come here and leave that for me. You'll like her. Trust me.

SHAZIA. I just don't think you've thought this through.

Silence.

Does Mum know?

Silence.

Does she speak English?

Silence.

How will you even support her?

ASHRAF. She will get allowance from me.

SHAZIA. Knew it.

ASHRAF. And when my sauce takes off she will work in the family business.

SHAZIA. Great. When *Dragon's Den* come knocking, yeah?

ASHRAF. You can have job too, Shazia – there's plenty to go round.

SHAZIA. I've got a job, Dad! Flogging a few bottles of peri peri on Wigan market isn't going to cut it. Does she want kids?

ASHRAF. Enough. I've got a headache. Let's talk about this another time –

SHAZIA. Yep. Just drop me off at mine.

ASHRAF. And it's not peri peri.

Scene Three

ASHRAF *is watching a video on his phone of a goat turning a tap on. The phone rings.* ASHRAF *picks up.*

JEAN. I hear congratulations are in order?

ASHRAF. What?

JEAN. Your new wife! Congratulations.

ASHRAF. Yes… well, it has been ten years, Jean –

JEAN. And don't I know it – you put me off men for life! Anyway, I just wanted to wish you good luck. And… Shazia seemed a bit, well… shocked. Was it, you know… arranged? She did know who she was getting, right?

ASHRAF. Course she bloody did! It is… how you say – one woman's trash is another woman's treasure.

(*Remembering to be offended.*) Anyway… this questioning is very rude!

JEAN. Well, look. Tell her to call me. You know, if she needs any advice.

ASHRAF. Oh yes, I'll be sure to give my new wife the direct line to my ex-wife, is Skype okay or do you prefer WhatsApp?

JEAN. I'm being serious. And next time you go bloody swanning off just give Shaz a call or something, she was worried sick.

ASHRAF. Yes, I know. She already had a go –

JEAN. Oh, and I picked up some fancy bottles for you from Lidls, you'll have to buy your own labels but they were on offer, honestly, you should get down there – four ninety-nine for twelve –

ASHRAF. Sorry – got another call coming –

He pushes the button to take the call.

As-salaam alaikum, brother!

YUSUF. Just letting you know I've put you on for double shifts next week okay?

ASHRAF. Which days? I have some meetings, *Inshallah*.

YUSUF. I told you this stupid sauce won't pay your bills. You want Yasmin to think you're a fool?

I have a pick-up for you in Aspull, I'm sending the details through now.

ASHRAF. Okay.

YUSUF. You spoken to Shazia yet?

ASHRAF. Not yet, I've been busy. I will.

YUSUF. I'm just looking out for you, you don't want people talking again.

ASHRAF. Yes, thank you.

YUSUF *hangs up.* ASHRAF *takes a fresh packet of fags out of his glovebox, lights up and starts the engine.*

Scene Four

ASHRAF *and* SHAZIA *are at the airport.*

ASHRAF. Where's your headscarf?

SHAZIA. I told you, she can meet me how I am.

ASHRAF. Here, put this on.

> ASHRAF *takes off a woolly tartan scarf.* SHAZIA *doesn't take it.*

Don't embarrass me –

SHAZIA. Just calm down.

> ASHRAF *checks his reflection in the window.*

ASHRAF. Pass me my brush.

> *She reaches into the glovebox and gets it out. He slicks down his remaining hair.*

Pass me a chewing gum.

SHAZIA. Normal, or Juicy Fruit.

ASHRAF. Normal. Pass me Joop.

> SHAZIA *gets it out and passes it over and* ASHRAF *begins spraying.*

SHAZIA. Go easy!

ASHRAF. Arab women like it. Look – you think I've lost weight?

SHAZIA. Since when?!

ASHRAF. I've lost weight, isn't it? Look I have – see?

SHAZIA. Yes, Dad. You lost weight. You look great.

ASHRAF. Good. Thank you.

> ASHRAF *checks his watch.*

Five minutes.

SHAZIA. Dad, there was something I wanted to say the other day, something I need to tell you –

ASHRAF. You'll like her, *habibi*. Trust me –

SHAZIA. Before she arrives we should talk about a few things –

ASHRAF. You will always be my *habibi*, my number one –

His phone beeps.

Where's the flowers?

SHAZIA *passes them to him.*

Okay. I'll be five minutes. Please, Shazia, just be...
respectful.

SHAZIA *takes the price tag off of the flowers and gives him
a kiss.*

SHAZIA. Good luck.

ASHRAF. Thanks, baby. (*Exits.*)

SHAZIA *calls* CHRIS.

SHAZIA. Hey – it's me, just in the cab waiting to meet Dad's
new wife... no biggie.

Pause.

Yeah, that sounds perfect, I need a night in.

(*Looking out the window to check they're not coming.
Whispering.*) Mmm... pepperoni? Love you... bye.

SHAZIA *picks up her dad's scarf and puts it on. She looks at
herself for a minute then freaks out and takes it off.*

ASHRAF *and* YASMIN *enter.*

ASHRAF. Shazia, this is Yasmin. (*To* YASMIN.) هذه شانيه
(*Hathithe Shazia.*) [This is Shazia.]

YASMIN (*to* ASHRAF). انها جميله (*'Iinaha jamila.*) [She is
beautiful.]

ASHRAF. She says you get your good looks from me.

YASMIN *goes to embrace* SHAZIA. *She kisses both her
cheeks and speaks in broken English.*

YASMIN. Very nice to meet you.

SHAZIA. Thank you! (*Shouting slowly*.) YOUR ENGLISH IS GOOD!

ASHRAF. She's not deaf, Shazia.

SHAZIA. So... good flight?

YASMIN. Pardon?

SHAZIA (*louder with a thumbs-up and an aeroplane gesture*). Good flight?

YASMIN. آه نعم شكراً. الموظفين كانت وديه للغايه وكان الطعم ممتاز ووصلنا في الوقت المحدد ما اكثر ما يمكن ان تريد.

(*Ahh nam. Shukraan. Almuazafin kanat wodiyah lilghaya, wakan altaem mumtaz,wa wasalna fi alwaqt almuhadad – ma 'akthar yomkin 'an turid!*) [Ah yes. Thank you. The staff were very friendly, the food was excellent and we landed on time – what more could you want!]

ASHRA (*translating*). Yes.

Silence.

SHAZIA. Who did you fly with?

ASHRAF. أي طيران؟ (*Ay tayaran.*) [Which airline?]

YASMIN. لماذا تسألين هذا؟ هناك أشياء اكثر اهميه. لقد تزوجنا للتو.

(*Limatha tas'alani hatha? Honakah 'ashya' 'akthar 'ahamiya? Lakad tazawajna liltow!*) [Why is she asking me this? There are more important things? We've just got married!]

ASHRAF. في إنجلترا يطلق عليها الحديث الصغير. سوف تتعلم انت محظوظا انها لا تتحدث علي الطقس .

(*Fi 'iingiltirah yotlaq alayha 'small talk' – sawfa tataalam. Kunt mahzuzaan 'anaha la tatahadath ala altaqs!*) [In England they call it 'small-talk' – you will learn. You're lucky she's not talking about the weather!]

YASMIN. Monarch.

SHAZIA. Aah – Monarch... every time I've flown with them they've been bloody late!

ASHRAF. Shazia, language!

YASMIN. ‏ماذا هي تقول؟‏ (*Matha hia taqul?*) [What is she saying?]

ASHRAF. ‏هي تقول انها سوف تاخذك الي قصر باكنغهام لمقابله (الملكة)‏ (*Wataqul 'iinaha sawfa takhudhuk 'iilaa qasr Buckingham –lemokapalat 'Monarch'*.) [She says she'll take you to Buckingham Palace – to meet our monarch.]

YASMIN. Thank you, Shazia.

SHAZIA. Er. That's fine? What is the weather like in Egypt?

ASHRAF. Hot.

SHAZIA. I was asking Yasmin!

ASHRAF. ‏الغسالة لها انكسرت .‏ (*Alghasala laha itkasarat.*) [Her washing machine broke.]

‏كما انها ارسلت الحجاب لها الي التنظيف .‏ (*Kama anah a arsalat alhijab laha illa altanzeef. Kol shay insarak.*) [She took her hijabs to the cleaner. Everything got stolen.]

SHAZIA. Dad. What are you saying? I know you're talking about me! Dad – ENGLISH!

YASMIN. I'm sorry to hear. Not good.

SHAZIA. About what?

ASHRAF. I was telling her what happened to your headscarves.

SHAZIA. Oh yeah?

ASHRAF. Yeah – you know that your washing machine broke, so you took them to the laundrette and someone stole all of your washing.

SHAZIA. Ah yeah. All of it. Gone. Bastards!

ASHRAF. Shazia – language.

YASMIN. ‏لديا العديد من الحجاب أستطيع ان اعطيك بعض اذا تريد.‏ (*Ladaya aladed min alhijab – 'astatea 'an 'oetik baed 'itha 'aradat?*) [I have many headscarves – I can give you some if you like?]

ASHRAF. She said that you should be covered up, and she's happy to lend you some headscarves.

SHAZIA. Thank you.

ASHRAF. In Arabic.

SHAZIA. Uh Shukran Yasmin.

YASMIN. You have dinner today?

SHAZIA. Oh no, I can't, I have to meet my boyfriend.

YASMIN. You have boyfriend?

> (*To* ASHRAF.) اشرف لماذا لم تخبريني . (*'Ashraf limatha lam tukhbirini?*) [Ashraf, why didn't you tell me?]

> (*To* SHAZIA.) He must come.

SHAZIA. Ah no. It's okay. He's at work till late but I said I would cook.

YASMIN. He is... new yes?

SHAZIA. No – four years.

YASMIN. Long time.

> (*To* ASHRAF.) لماذا لم تلتقي بيه ؟ وهذا ليس جيد. وهذا هو اشرف رهيب يجب ان تلتقي هذا الرجل.

> (*Limatha lam altaqayat bih, wahathan laysa jayidan, wahatha hoa 'Ashraf rahyb. yajib 'an taltaqi haetha alrajol!?*) [Why haven't you met him, this is not good. This is terrible, Ashraf. You must meet this man!?]

> (*To* SHAZIA.) Shazia, we all have meeting? Soon? Please – not good that Ashraf not met...?

SHAZIA. Chris.

YASMIN. Yes, Chris. So yes we –

ASHRAF. اسمين لا انهم مشغولون جدا. أنا مشغولة مع العمل. (*Yasmin, la 'anahum mashghulun jiddn. 'Ana mashghula maeh alahmal –*) [Yasmin, no they're very busy. I am busy with work –]

YASMIN. اشرف عائلته أسره الأسره هي رقم واحد. (*Ashraf ayilatuh. 'Usra. Al'usra hi raqm wahid.*) [Ashraf, it's family. Family. Family is number one.] Shazia you come to the house.

SHAZIA. Or we could go for a drink at The Star... bucks, on Wigan Lane. You know, have a latte or a frappomochachino – ever had one of those, Yasmin? They're great... or a muffin. But I won't have a muffin 'cause I don't really eat cake. And no er –

ASHRAF. Any place you like.

SHAZIA. Okay?

ASHRAF (*proudly*). This. Is my taxi.

Scene Five

ASHRAF *is in the driver's seat and* YASMIN *is in the passenger seat.* YASMIN *is leaning down and looking at* ASHRAF*'s feet.*

ASHRAF. Watch! Watch – are you watching?

YASMIN. Yes.

ASHRAF. You see my right one goes down, and the left eases up. See?

YASMIN. Yes.

ASHRAF. So show me.

YASMIN. ‏ليس لدي أي دواسات هنا ممكن اقعد مكانك.‏ (*Laysa ladaya 'ayu dawasat huna. Momkin ackaud makanak –*) [I don't have any pedals here. Can't I –]

ASHRAF. In English.

YASMIN. No. Pedals.

ASHRAF. Just imagine you have pedals.

YASMIN. Imagine.

ASHRAF. Right.

YASMIN. Okay. So I push down –

ASHRAF. Smoothly. Smoothly! You can't be jerking like that!

YASMIN. It *is* smoothly. There's no pedals – how do you know if it's smoothly!

ASHRAF. I can see, okay – I have eyes!

YASMIN. You also have brain, but you still only drive taxi for living.

ASHRAF. At the moment – you wait until my business –

YASMIN. 'Your business' this, 'your business' that – how is it you say? More trousers, less talk, yes?

ASHRAF. Well, just you remember who is wearing the trousers here, okay?

YASMIN. They will not fit very long if you keep with these pies!

ASHRAF. Go again. Smoothly.

YASMIN. I do it on the pedals. Engine off.

ASHRAF. Fine.

They switch seats.

YASMIN. Like this?

ASHRAF. Yes. Keep going. Twenty times at least.

YASMIN. Right.

ASHRAF *gets some flashcards out of his pocket.*

ASHRAF. King Henry VIII's daughter Mary was a devout Catholic and persecuted Protestants, which is why she became known as: A) Catholic Mary, B) Killer Mary, C) Bloody Mary, or D) There's Something About Mary.

YASMIN. She was Catholic. 'A' please. Catholic Mary.

ASHRAF. No. Not good. Your English is coming but if you want to live here you must blend in. Mix and blend. Smoothly – smoothly!

YASMIN. Okay!

ASHRAF*'s phone rings – he picks up.*

Brother. Where are you?

ASHRAF. It's my day off, yes? I'm teaching Yasmin to drive!

YUSUF. In the taxi?

ASHRAF. Er... No – just theory.

YUSUF. We were expecting you at mosque.

ASHRAF. Ah – sorry – completely slipped my mind.

YUSUF. And will Shazia be coming later with Yasmin? Omar wants her to meet his son. Very good match.

ASHRAF. I told you already – no dowry, no Shazia.

YUSUF. They're working on it. Hafifah has some things for Yasmin – she will bring them. Hey – you get that video of the goat and the tap?

ASHRAF. Yes, brother! Such a good one! I have one of a goat squealing like a human that I will send you later.

YUSUF. Shukraan.

ASHRAF. Right.

ASHRAF *hangs up the phone. Gets out another card.*

Pubs are usually open from A) 8.00 a.m., B) 9.00 a.m., C) 10.00 a.m., D) 11.00 a.m.

YASMIN. I don't believe in pubs.

ASHRAF. For the English, pubs is like mosque.

YASMIN. All this drinking is shameful.

ASHRAF. You must never say that in Wigan.

YASMIN. No wonder they end up with Killer Queen Mary – she was probably one over the arse of a rat.

ASHRAF. Smoothly!

YASMIN. And speaking of rats you also need to tell Yusuf to stick it where it's dark outside yes?

ASHRAF. Right, two more questions then you sing National Anthem.

Scene Six

Late at night, SHAZIA *is drunk, standing on the side of the road, crying and mumbling as* ASHRAF *screeches in.*

ASHRAF. Get in. Get in before anybody sees! What time do you call this?

SHAZIA *sits on the kerb.* ASHRAF *reluctantly gets out.*

Where is your coat? It's bloody freezing!

SHAZIA. S'over.

ASHRAF. What are you saying? Speak English. Are you drunk?

SHAZIA (*thinking for a minute*). Yes.

ASHRAF. عار عليكي شانيه. (*Aar alayike Shazia.*) [Shame on you, Shazia.]

Silence.

Were you spiked?

SHAZIA. No.

ASHRAF. So this is it? You're drinking alcohol now?

Silence.

Shazia?

Silence.

Shazia, be honest with me. I am your father. Respect at all times. Are you drinking alcohol now?

SHAZIA (*snapping*). Aaargh! YES! Well not *now*, exactly… been getting wasted most weekends for, let me count… one, two, five… nine years! Thought you might have had an inkling?

ASHRAF. You're practically naked. Never mind your hair – I can see your arms, your legs –

SHAZIA. You don't have to look.

ASHRAF. What's happened to you, *habibi*?

SHAZIA. Nothing's happened! Dad! This is me. Deal with it, okay?

ASHRAF. No. You're a good Muslim girl, this is not how you were brought up –

SHAZIA. How would you know?

ASHRAF. You're better than this. This isn't you.

SHAZIA. You don't know me! You know a version of me. The version I think you can handle. I'm still never good enough though, am I? Even on my best fucking behavior, there's always something –

ASHRAF. This swearing –

SHAZIA. Oh, pray for me, Dad. I'm gonna need it – seem to be racking up a hell of a lot of shame. *Haram! Haram!*

Suddenly she bursts into tears. He takes a breath. He pulls her close and hugs her.

ASHRAF. What happened?

SHAZIA *starts twisting and pulling at her engagement ring.*

SHAZIA. It's over. The wedding's off.

ASHRAF (*exploding*). Wedding?! I've never even met him!

SHAZIA. Wonder where I learned that.

Silence.

ASHRAF. You should have told me.

SHAZIA. I tried.

ASHRAF. Not very hard.

SHAZIA. I thought you'd disapprove.

ASHRAF. I do.

SHAZIA. Well I'm hardly ecstatic about Yas... how much is she getting again? Wish I could sit about doing fuck-all!

SHAZIA *stares into space. She starts to weep again.*

ASHRAF. What has that pig-fucker son of a donkey done to you? Did he hit you?

SHAZIA. No.

ASHRAF. You know if I find out he hit you, I'll castrate that cow-licking bastard.

SHAZIA. He didn't hit me.

ASHRAF. He cheat on you? Eh? My beautiful daughter not enough for that pimp whore?

SHAZIA. No. He didn't cheat on me.

ASHRAF. So what? What is so bad that this 'wedding' is off?

SHAZIA. He went home.

ASHRAF. And?

SHAZIA. And he tried to make me go with him.

ASHRAF. So you are still living separately? *Alhamdu lellah!*

SHAZIA. No. We live together.

Silence. He lights up a cigarette.

You know that's harming yourself?

ASHRAF. I think of it more like preserving – like a smoked salmon. Anyway you can talk – you're blind like a bat drunk!

SHAZIA. Oh no no no – it's more like preserving... like a pickled egg.

Silence. They both laugh.

ASHRAF. Come. Get in, it's cold.

ASHRAF *helps her up and into the cab.*

So tell me, my 'pickled egg', what is so wrong with him wanting to go home and you go home too?

SHAZIA. I was having fun! It was my choice! Just 'cause he's a boring old fart doesn't mean I have to be!

ASHRAF. So you don't do as he tells you either.

SHAZIA. No, Dad! I don't do as anyone tells me! I'm a grown woman, not a possession and I'll do what I fucking well like!

ASHRAF. Well, as long as you fucking well swear I'm sure he'll bloody fucking get the dogshit message.

She laughs.

SHAZIA. It's the principle – it was like I didn't have a say. And... and then... what else might I not have a say in? I am not a fucking pet – I'm an independent woman!

(*Deciding.*) Nope. It's over. This can't go on.

ASHRAF. You're right, *habibi*. This is a wake-up call. No good man would let you out like this.

SHAZIA. *Let* me?!

ASHRAF. Yes – he should have more pride – not want everyone to see what he has.

SHAZIA. Oh my God! This is what I'm saying –

ASHRAF. And after four years with no marriage – this is not taking you seriously.

SHAZIA. We are getting married! Well... we were.

This brings on a new wave of emotion from SHAZIA.

ASHRAF. You must stick to your own faith, your own culture –

SHAZIA. He is my culture – well, half at least anyway –

ASHRAF. This is what happens. Now you have lived with him. Some sins are hard to reverse, you –

SHAZIA. But you married Mum –

ASHRAF. So you are lucky now to learn from my mistake. That 'half' culture – Bloody Cilla Black and Mister Blobby – is why you are in this situation at all. Right. So where should I take you then?

SHAZIA. I'm guessing you won't take me back to Mum's?

ASHRAF. To Preston? Now?

More crying from SHAZIA. *A deep breath from* ASHRAF.

They pull up at ASHRAF's *house.* ASHRAF *gets out to* YASMIN *waiting at the door in her dressing gown.* SHAZIA *stays in the cab.*

YASMIN. ماذا يحدث هنا. (*Matha yahduth hunnah?*) [What's going on?]

ASHRAF. It's Shazia. She's drunk, she has no clothes on and she's crying because she's had a fight with this boyfriend who she lives with.

YASMIN. He hit her?

ASHRAF. No no, nothing like that.

A beat.

I should disown her.

YASMIN. She is a grown woman – you don't own her in the first place.

A beat.

ASHRAF. She shouldn't have a boyfriend anyway. People have seen her. It's best that they split up. Then I can find her a nice Muslim husband. She's a disgrace.

YASMIN. اشرف لقد كانت اربع سنوات معا ولم تكن قد قابلته انت عار ويجب عليك تعلم الولاء والعمل من خلال المشاكل.

(*Ashraf. Laqad kanat arba sanawat maan walam takun qad qabaltaho. 'Ant aar. Wayajib 'alaika taealahm alwala' walehlamal min khilal almashakil –*) [Ashraf. They have been four years together and you haven't even met him. You are the disgrace. And shouldn't you teach loyalty and working through problems –]

ASHRAF. No – I teach don't have a dogshit Western boyfriend… no, fiancé, who lets you out half naked!

YASMIN. They're engaged?

ASHRAF. Not if I have anything to do with it.

YASMIN *peers round to see what* SHAZIA*'s doing.*

YASMIN. Don't you feel sorry for her?

ASHRAF. She has made her bed.

YASMIN. You've never made a mistake? Am I not your *second* wife?! دعونا نحصل عليها انظر عليها (*Daeuna nahsul alayha. Onzur laha.*) [Let's get her in. Look after her.]

ASHRAF. No! I am not letting that shame through my door.

YASMIN. Goodnight, Ashraf. You are the shame not coming through this door. You ring the bell when this is better.

انت لن تعود في هذا البيت حتي يتم ذلك.

(*'Anta lan taeoud fi hatha albaiyt hatta yatim thalik.*) [You're not coming back in this house until it's done.]

He storms back to the cab and sits in the driver's seat. He takes his beads off the mirror and looks at them a while. Long pause.

ASHRAF. Listen to me, Shazia. This Carl?

SHAZIA. Chris.

ASHRAF. Chris. What was his intention? Did he intend to prove you were his possession by behaving in that way?

SHAZIA. I guess not.

ASHRAF. What then?

SHAZIA. I guess he thought I'd had enough, probably wouldn't remember the last hour anyway, would regret staying, feel shit tomorrow and not do what I'd promised myself which was go to yoga.

ASHRAF. Want some advice from me?

SHAZIA. Why not?

ASHRAF. Marry him.

SHAZIA. Really?

ASHRAF (*retracting*). I need to meet him of course.

Pause.

I guess it won't be a Muslim wedding?

SHAZIA *shakes her head.*

He should at least have asked for my permission – I will be telling him this.

SHAZIA. You were in Egypt? Untraceable? Getting married?

A pause.

ASHRAF. Do you remember when I used to take you to that stables?

SHAZIA. Ha, yes! And that fucking horse kicked me in the face!

ASHRAF. So you swore to tame it and have it pull you in a carriage to your wedding!

SHAZIA. Ha! Yeah… don't think we can really stretch to horses, maybe a tandem or something!

ASHRAF. You will have the horses and the carriage. That will be my gift.

SHAZIA. No, Dad really, it's fine, save your money –

ASHRAF. Do not question me, you are still my daughter! Respect for parents at all times –

In all of this, ASHRAF's *coat has come undone and she sees his PJs. He sheepishly does up his buttons.*

SHAZIA. Dad?

ASHRAF. Yes.

SHAZIA. Sorry Yasmin had to see me like this. She must be disgusted.

ASHRAF. She'll get over it.

Scene Seven

SHAZIA *goes to get in the front of the cab but* ASHRAF *locks that door from inside and winds the window down a bit. He gestures for her to get in the back. She doesn't. He winds it down a bit more to speak.*

ASHRAF. Get in the back.

SHAZIA (*getting into the back*). Yep, great start. Why do I have to get in the back?

ASHRAF. No headscarf. We agreed – Yasmin is coming.

SHAZIA. But –

ASHRAF. So now I will have Kev in the front.

SHAZIA. His name is Chris!

ASHRAF. Chris, will ride with me to the restaurant. And you will get to know Yasmin some more.

SHAZIA. Please don't be embarrassing.

ASHRAF. Ditto.

SHAZIA. You've got loads in common... music, football –

ASHRAF. Wigan Athletic?

SHAZIA. Man U.

ASHRAF spits in disgust.

It's a game. Do you know where you're going?

ASHRAF. First we pick up him, and then we get Yasmin and then to the restaurant, yes?

SHAZIA. Right. It's the next right.

ASHRAF. I am aware of this, Shazia, I drive taxi for my profession.

ASHRAF pulls over. CHRIS is already waiting, smiling and waving, wearing a suit.

SHAZIA. Smile, Dad. Please.

ASHRAF gruffly beckons CHRIS into the front seat next to him.

ASHRAF. Come.

As CHRIS gets in, ASHRAF shuts the glass between the front and back seats.

CHRIS. Alakazam, Ashraf, pleased to meet you.

ASHRAF. *As-salaam alaikum.*

(*With a cheeky grin.*) Kyle. Pleased to meet you.

SHAZIA starts banging on the window. ASHRAF slides it open a crack.

What is it?

SHAZIA. I just think we should all talk together.

ASHRAF. You talk too much.

CHRIS. Fair point!

ASHRAF. Do not disrespect her. Let me and Chris talk as men. And when Yasmin comes you can talk as women. About nails and Brian Gosling and suchlike.

SHAZIA. This is ridiculous.

ASHRAF *shuts the window.*

ASHRAF. You plan to marry my daughter.

CHRIS. Er yes. Yeah, I mean, I'd love to, if that's okay with you?

ASHRAF. Will she be wearing purdah once you are wed?

CHRIS. Purdah. Er. Yeah, I'm sure she'd look great in er... purdah.

ASHRAF. Good. And if you have children will they go to mosque?

CHRIS. I mean... that's quite a way off I think – Shaz, er... Shazia wants to focus on her career for a while first so –

ASHRAF. You will not be providing for her?

CHRIS. Oh, er, yes, yes of course I will, just, she's... well, she's very clever and wants to pursue her career –

ASHRAF. I see you have a good Muslim beard.

CHRIS. Yep. Yes I do...

Silence. SHAZIA *starts to bang on the window again.*

ASHRAF. Just ignore. She will tire. We can drown out.

ASHRAF *puts the radio on – some of his classic Arabic tunes. It's 'Ana Mosh Kaafir' ('I'm Not a Heathen') by Ziad Rahbani.* CHRIS *starts nodding his head along.*

You like Arab music? Rahbani?

CHRIS. Oh yeah, yeah, he's great – really catchy.

ASHRAF *pulls over –* YASMIN *is waiting at the side.*

ASHRAF. Yes, this is one of Shazia's favourites – translated means 'I am not a heathen'.

YASMIN *appears at* CHRIS*'s window in a headscarf.* CHRIS *winds it down.*

YASMIN. You are Chris! We have heard about you. *As-salaam alaikum.*

CHRIS *puts his hand out of the window to go for a formal handshake.*

CHRIS. Hi, Yasmin. It's a pleasure.

YASMIN. Let's go.

YASMIN *gets in the car.*

How are you, Ashraf? Good day?

SHAZIA. He's got the window shut. He wanted to talk to Chris without me apparently.

YASMIN. Oh dear.

SHAZIA. I'm sorry I've got my hair out.

YASMIN. You look nice.

CHRIS. So… Shaz says you like the footie?

ASHRAF. Yes I do. How many Man U supporters does it take to stop a moving bus?

CHRIS. Er –

ASHRAF. Never enough. What do you call a Manchester person with no arms and legs?

CHRIS. Parapleg–

ASHRAF. Trustworthy. What's the difference between a dead fox in the road and a dead Manchester fan?

CHRIS. I think this is a bit –

ASHRAF (*cracking up at himself*). Skid marks in front of the fox! Ha!

A beat.

Go on then. Your turn. You must have a joke? You like to laugh?

CHRIS. Nah, you're alright.

ASHRAF. Come on, man! Even Shazia has good jokes! Anything?

CHRIS. Alright, alright – if we're okay with doing *personal* jokes how about this... how does a Muslim close the door?

ASHRAF. My religion is not –

CHRIS. Islams it! Get it?! Islam? He slams?!

YASMIN *taps on the window.* ASHRAF *opens it a bit.*

YASMIN. Let's all talk together no? I want to meet Chris.

ASHRAF. Oh okay yes. Chris, why don't you tell my wife the joke you just made about Islam?

CHRIS. Nah, mate, you're alright. You've given away the punchline now anyway.

YASMIN. Chris, Shazia says you are teacher? Children with special needs?

CHRIS. That's right.

YASMIN. Very difficult.

CHRIS. Nah, it's great really. Got a funny bunch at the moment. This one lad's got a feeding tube up his nose, and I've got another one with a sort of fetish for tubes – keeps trying to pull it out – constantly chasing after him making tracks round the classroom. Luckily the one with the tube is a bit faster 'cause he's got a dead posh supersonic-wheelchair thing – like Lewis Hamilton he is... broom broom!!

YASMIN. This must be how you manage the sadness! Humour very important! Yes! This is how I deal with Ashraf! As they say 'laughter is better than the drugs'.

ASHRAF (*quickly changing the subject*). How were your studies today? Still struggling?

CHRIS. Studies?

YASMIN. Yes – I had been studying my driving theory. But I have some good news.

CHRIS. Go on?

YASMIN. I passed! Today. At the test centre!

ASHRAF. You didn't tell me you booked the test.

YASMIN. I didn't want to disappoint if I fail.

SHAZIA. Yasmin, that's amazing!

ASHRAF. Yes – Yasmin has been here three months and passed. What is your excuse?

CHRIS. I'm teaching her.

SHAZIA. Yeah, I even went round the car park the other day didn't I?

ASHRAF. Car park and Mesnes Park very different… and don't get me started on Saddle Junction –

YASMIN. You will get there, Shazia.

SHAZIA. You know, your English is so much better, Yas–

YASMIN. I have the citizenship test next.

CHRIS. You'll be fine – your English is great!

YASMIN. Thank you but the English is not it. I need to know about Henry 8th daughter – the Bloody Mary –

ASHRAF. Yasmin!

CHRIS. That's her name –

ASHRAF. You must not defend this language –

YASMIN. And for how many years you defend against Romans, and what bird you eat on your Christmas festival –

ASHRAF. Turkey of course – this is easy.

YASMIN. Oh yes – how you say? A slice of the cake?

CHRIS. Thinking about it though, some people like a ham on Christmas Day –

SHAZIA. Chris!

CHRIS. What?

SHAZIA. We don't eat ham!

CHRIS. You don't celebrate Christmas either!

ASHRAF. Someone has to drive the drunk idiots on Christmas Day!

CHRIS. Seriously though – no bacon? You don't know what you're missing!

SHAZIA. Chris!

CHRIS. What?!

ASHRAF. Swine is unclean, haram.

CHRIS. Yeah, probably if you hang it up in the desert heat for five days, but if you get it from the cold counter at Lidl it –

SHAZIA. For fuck's sake, Chris!

Scene Eight

A notification beeps on ASHRAF*'s phone, he sees it and hurriedly turns on the radio.*

RADIO.…Reports of a bomb blast at Manchester Airport – so far seven are reported dead and many injured in what is thought to be a clear act of Islamist terrorism.

The bomber is described as of Middle Eastern descent and reports suggest he shouted '*Allahu Akbar*' meaning 'God is great' before the bomb was detonated.

ASHRAF *turns off the radio, agitated.*

ASHRAF. This is not Islam.

He picks up the phone to call YASMIN.

Salaam. Have you seen the news? (*Pause.*) I know I know, these stupid pig-licking dumb waiters making it harder.

(*Pause.*) Sorry. Look. Don't leave the house. (*Pause.*) No,
I'll pick up some later, it can wait. Please promise me.
(*Pause.*) Okay. Okay. Yasmin but please if you do go, don't
wear your scarf. I don't mind. This one time... it's not safe
okay? Okay *salaam salaam*. (*Pause.*) And get me some
biscuits... Bourbons, or Dark Chocolate Hobnobs. Yes. Just
one more pick up then I'll be home.

ASHRAF *lights a fag and turns on the engine.*

Scene Nine

A string of calls going into voicemails – people can't get hold of
ASHRAF.

VOICEMAIL 1 – YUSUF. Brother – where are you? Call me
back.

VOICEMAIL 2 – YUSUF. Ashraf. Pick up the phone, man. We
need to talk.

VOICEMAIL 3 – YUSUF. I'm serious. I have letters here. Two
car payments missed? So this is how you repay me? All
these meetings means less shifts and missed payments. Call
me right now!

VOICEMAIL 4 – JEAN. Now listen, I was chatting to Joan the
other day and her nephew Charlie who works for this fast-
food place. I were telling 'im about your sauce and he were
dead interested. So next time you see Shaz give her a few
bottles for me and I'll pass it on. And I won't ask for
commission 'cause Shaz worries about you anyway, but
don't say I never do anything for you, eh? And how's the
new wife? Enjoying picking up your hundreds of half-drunk
coffee mugs? Anyway, just gimme a bell when –

*The machine beeps her out because she's been talking too
long.*

Scene Ten

ASHRAF *has been beaten up and his cab is in tatters. He falls out of the cab onto the pavement outside his house, breathing heavily. He takes a moment to try and smarten himself up.*
YASMIN *comes out.*

YASMIN. يا عزيزتي ماذا حدث.   (*Ya azizaty! Matha hadath?*) [My darling! What happened?]

ASHRAF. I'm sorry.

YASMIN. ماذا حدث   (*Matha hadath?*) [What happened?]

ASHRAF. It's fine. I will be fine it –

YASMIN. أرجوك   (*Arjouk.*) [Please.]

A beat.

ASHRAF. They. They got in the cab. Wanted to go to The Gerrard Arms in Aspull. They said I wasn't their mate. They call me Mohammad. I said I am good person and to please calm down. They asked me what I thought about the bomb in the airport. I said, I said any killing is bad. They said I was friends with ISIS, that I should go back to Syria and that they would burn me and stuff my face with bacon. I ask them to leave the taxi. I try to film it, to stop them – make them leave. They drag me out of the taxi and start to smash, cut the seats. I try to pull one off and he slams my eye with his elbow. I am hurt and they are big, strong men. There is nothing I can do. I have to stand there while they destroy my... my business, my life.

Silence.

I am so sorry, Yasmin.

YASMIN. أرجوك سوف تكون علي ما يرام.   (*Arjouk. Sawfa takun alaa ma youraum –*)[Please. You will be okay, you mustn't –]

ASHRAF. I should not have brought you here for this. I have nothing to offer –

YASMIN. That is not true! You have shared everything with me –

ASHRAF. It's not enough. You deserve better. I am old... weak –

YASMIN. No, you deserve better. That taxi is not your life and neither are those stupid men. I am and Shazia is. These pigs can rot in their own shit. We will mend taxi, your eye will mend, and when you are on top of your feet we will launch your business. Together.

Pause.

Come, Ashraf – you are practically British – what do they say? Keep the calm and carry it on. We must carry. Stiff lips. Six months we will be Richard Branson. Yes?

Pause.

Yes?

ASHRAF. As long as you know that I am the boss.

YASMIN. Yes. Now let's get you inside, boss man.

ASHRAF. Thank you.

YASMIN. You are hero.

Scene Eleven

We see YASMIN *approach the car with a hand-held vacuum and cleaning products. She is tidying up after the attack. There's glass everywhere and the car is a state. She takes a moment to look around the car.*

YASMIN. Ashraf… my days. God was looking down on you.

There are mugs everywhere. She starts trying to stack them. She finds an old plastic bag and makes a bin.

How many? Never heard of washing up?

The same happens with old copies of The Sun. *She reads a headline out loud.*

'Girl Sues KitKat for "Emotional Damage" as she's left Waferless.'

She picks up another paper.

'Gordon Ramsay Sex Dwarf Eaten by Badger.' What is this trash?

She turns the page – sees the page-three girl staring back at her.

'Lola says the tax on sugar is another example of the nanny state at work.'

Pause.

I think Lola is needs a nanny. To help her remember her clothes in the morning.

She stuffs the papers into a bin bag then reaches under his chair to find empty boxes of cigarettes stuffed under the seat.

'Yasmin, believe me... I stop smoking. Believe me!' Lies! And I can smell the Joop. You think I'm stupid?

She gets out gaffer tape and begins to mend the ripped seats. She has made covers to make the car look nice.

She wipes down the taxi radio and accidentally switches it on and can hear YUSUF *talking to other people. She sits in the driver's seat and pretends to pick up a passenger.*

Where you off to, mate? No problems... you having a nice day? The weather is nice...

She gets out ASHRAF's *prayer beads from her pocket and puts them back up proudly on the mirror.*

Scene Twelve

We see YASMIN *in the driver's seat of the taxi. She is tying her headscarf into more of a modern style, like a bun. She applies her lipstick and her phone rings.*

YASMIN. *Habibi*, I'm outside.

SHAZIA *gets into the car.*

SHAZIA. *As-salaam alaikum.* I didn't expect you to be driving.

YASMIN. Yes, now I passed, here I am on the insurance.

SHAZIA. Great.

YASMIN. When your dad is better he will teach you.

SHAZIA. Erm… no. Better?

YASMIN. Yes… this is why I call you.

SHAZIA. What's wrong with him?

YASMIN. He had some bad people in his taxi.

SHAZIA. What?

YASMIN. Don't worry. He is 'in the mend'.

SHAZIA. What did they do? I'll kill them. Why didn't he tell me? When did this happen? Why didn't you call me?

YASMIN. Please, we didn't want you to worry. He is okay.

SHAZIA. What did they do?

YASMIN. They smash the windows and with a key cut the seats.

SHAZIA. Was it racist? Was it a racist attack? Is he hurt?

YASMIN. He is lucky, believe me, but his eye is bad and he can't drive.

SHAZIA *wells up.*

SHAZIA. Fucking dipshit dumbass uneducated fuck-stains. Did you go to the police?

YASMIN. Yes, but they have not found them yet. Don't worry. God will have his plans for them.

Silence.

SHAZIA. What will you do for money? Do you need help? Look, I can go to the cash machine –

YASMIN. No.

SHAZIA. But how will you –

YASMIN. We have some donations through – from the mosque – see – religion is like family, it –

SHAZIA. But that won't last long will it, how will you –

The radio crackles.

Wait… you're not driving this thing, are you?

Silence.

Yasmin?

YASMIN. It's fine. I have driver's licence and sat nav. It's good… I'm getting to know Wigan.

SHAZIA. What? You don't have a taxi licence. You can't just pick up people. And are you actually insured on this car?

YASMIN. It's okay. As long as we have a good heart, God will protect us.

SHAZIA. Okay… I'm not sure if the police will see it that way. I don't think I can let you do this.

YASMIN. Too late.

SHAZIA. How late?

YASMIN. Two days. I make very good money.

SHAZIA. But –

YASMIN. It needed to replace windscreen and windows… we must to make some money to pay back. So when your father is better he can come straight back to taxi.

SHAZIA. I can't believe he let you do this!

A look.

He doesn't know?!

YASMIN. I save – for his spicy sauce. I spoke to Wigan market for a pitch.

Pause.

He is too good for this taxi.

Pause.

I believe the saying is 'what he doesn't know didn't kill him'. I can trust you. Yes?

SHAZIA. Yes. And while we're telling secrets… I never wear a headscarf. And I don't pray. I don't even know the proper prayer thing.

YASMIN. What? This is bad. We must take you to the mosque to pray for forgiveness. Straight away.

A beat.

Shazia, I don't care. You are my family. I know all this anyway... your father is bad liar!

The radio crackles. We hear YUSUF *talking to a different driver about a job.*

Right, now we pick up Mr Patel – let's get him before whoever Yusuf sends. As the saying goes 'one bird in hand is worth two big bushes'.

Both of their phones go at the same time. It's a video from ASHRAF *of a goat with a monkey riding on its back.*

Scene Thirteen

ASHRAF *is sitting on the street next to the cab, smoking. He has an eye patch on and looks terrible.* CHRIS *approaches.*

ASHRAF. I am busy.

CHRIS. Peace offering. Breakfast.

He hands over what looks like a bacon sandwich.

ASHRAF. Is this some sort of sick joke?

CHRIS. What? No no! Got it from Oliver Twist's. It's facon. Facon. Fake bacon?

ASHRAF. Yes?

CHRIS. Yep! All the goodness of bacon, none of the shame.

ASHRAF. Are you sure?

CHRIS. Er yeah.

ASHRAF. Then why not sell this in the halal shops?

CHRIS. Well, it's not meat, is it? It's more for the beardy vegans I think.

ASHRAF. Nothing wrong with beards.

CHRIS. I know. Try it then!

ASHRAF. Okay.

He bites into it.

CHRIS. Is it rank? Sorry. Should've known it'd be –

ASHRAF. No – no! Wait, it just needs something a little extra, hang on!

He goes to his car and gets out a pot of his sauce and pours it on.

Delicious. It just needed Ashraf's special sauce! I should sell this at the mosque – would make a killing! Facon Butties. Spicy Facon. Finger Lickin' Facon. Take On Some Facon.

CHRIS. Facon Fac-off?

ASHRAF. What?

CHRIS. Never mind.

ASHRAF. Right.

CHRIS. Ashraf. There was something I wanted to ask, something I should have asked a long time ago.

ASHRAF. Yes?

CHRIS. Would it be okay if I married Shaz? With you I mean. Do I have your permission?

ASHRAF. Does she know you're here?

CHRIS. Er… no.

ASHRAF. She would say the permission is not for me to give.

CHRIS. Yeah. Yeah she would.

ASHRAF. But since she's not here, then I will consider it.

CHRIS. What?

ASHRAF. Just my little joke. You have the permission.

CHRIS. Thanks. I am sorry about the whole Christmas-ham thing. I didn't know it was such a big deal.

ASHRAF. The Manchester United is more of a concern.

CHRIS. Here's one. What does a Wigan Athletic fan do when his team wins the league?

ASHRAF. Take his rightful place in history –

CHRIS. Turn off the PlayStation!

ASHRAF. Bloody dickhead.

Scene Fourteen

ASHRAF *is sat in the same spot. Still can't drive, still not healed. There's a collection of stuff around him – mugs, wrappers, fag butts, etc.*

ASHRAF *calls a number and we hear it ring.*

VOICE ONE. Hello, Cinderella Carriage Hire – may I help?

ASHRAF. Oh hello. I'm wondering if I can get a quote for a wedding.

VOICE ONE. No problem, what month are we looking at?

ASHRAF. August.

VOICE ONE. And the length of the journey?

ASHRAF. About fifteen minutes.

VOICE ONE. Right okay, let me see. Well, of course, we have to book you in for an hour minimum – with a standard carriage, that'll be approximately one thousand, eight hundred pounds.

ASHRAF. What? What if we get rid of a horse?

VOICE ONE. Excuse me?

ASHRAF. Just one horse – I don't mind. And it can be an old one.

VOICE ONE. I'm very sorry, sir – it doesn't work like that.

ASHRAF. And if we don't have the man? I'll ride the horse.

VOICE ONE. Well, firstly, nobody's riding them, and legally we have to send one of our professional handlers out.

ASHRAF. I have much experience with horses. In the seventies my father –

VOICE ONE. Very sorry – it's a legal requirement.

ASHRAF. Any discount? Please? I promised my daughter.

VOICE ONE. I'm afraid not. It's also a peak month.

ASHRAF. Okay, okay, I compromise. Do you have any donkeys?

VOICE ONE *hangs up*.

Hello? Hello?

ASHRAF *takes his beads off the mirror. He hesitates before he picks up his phone and dials another number.*

YUSUF. *As-salaam alaikum*, Ashraf.

ASHRAF. *Alaikum salaam.* How are you?

YUSUF. I should be asking you this. How is your eye? Have you been resting?

ASHRAF. I'm wondering if you can do me a favour, brother?

YUSUF. Anything.

ASHRAF. Well, you know I haven't been working. And I know I owe you already, believe me, but it's Shazia's wedding soon and I just need some help – a small loan for… just a few hundred. Of course I would pay it all back.

YUSUF. I am very surprised at you asking me this.

ASHRAF. What?

YUSUF. You say you are Muslim.

ASHRAF. Yes.

YUSUF. This wedding is forbidden – big sin, shame. And you dare to ask me to bring myself into this situation? To compromise my faith?

ASHRAF. Please, brother, it's for Shazia, your niece – family.

YUSUF. You are no brother. This wedding must not be permitted. I urge you in the name of Allah.

ASHRAF. Right. Thank you for your time anyway.

YUSUF. This Western man is no good for Shazia.

ASHRAF. You haven't met him.

YUSUF. And if you don't do the right thing, you will face consequences.

ASHRAF. Of course.

ASHRAF *hangs up and takes a minute. He calls* SHAZIA.

SHAZIA. Hi, Dad, how are you feeling now? Your eye?

ASHRAF. Hey, baby, good – much better. How are you?

SHAZIA. Good. A bit stressed – starting to think making one thousand paper cranes wasn't such good luck after all!

ASHRAF. Those bloody cranes – you roped in Yasmin too! Our house is full!

SHAZIA. Sorry, Dad! Is everything okay at your end?

ASHRAF. The horse and cart… it's… it's all booked. The one you wanted!

SHAZIA. Aah – amazing! Thanks, Dad, it's a dream come true.

ASHRAF. Anyway, I've got to go, I'll call you later.

ASHRAF *hangs up and searches on his phone, dials.*

VOICE TWO. Hello – welcome to Bonga Loans. May I take your name please?

ASHRAF. Mr Abd El Hakim.

VOICE TWO. And how can I help you today Mr Abd El Hakim?

YASMIN *goes out to the cab – he sees her.*

ASHRAF. Forget it. You are leeches off the poor and needy. I work bloody hard for my money.

ASHRAF *hangs up.*

Scene Fifteen

YASMIN *is in the taxi. We hear* YUSUF *say something about The Galleries,* YASMIN *fires up the engine. Her phone rings, she picks up.*

YASMIN. Yusuf.

YUSUF. Yasmin, good, I was hoping to speak to you at mosque but you left so quickly.

YASMIN. Yes – I needed to get back to Ashraf – he's still very sore.

YUSUF. Right.

YASMIN. Right.

YUSUF. When do you think he'll be driving again?

YASMIN. Tomorrow. He is determined. It is too soon, but he is stubborn.

YUSUF. You need to talk to him, Yasmin.

YASMIN. I do – every day!

YUSUF. About this wedding. You know it's *haram*.

YASMIN. Shazia is not a practising Muslim.

YUSUF. Even worse. We will lose her for good if this happens.

YASMIN. Who is this 'we'.

YUSUF. You'll have to disown her. It will be hard but we will be here for you.

YASMIN. Another 'we'.

YUSUF. There are things you don't know, Yasmin. I have had to support Ashraf financially. That taxi –

YASMIN. I do know, Yusuf. I know he's paying installments to you. I know he's been struggling to make payments. I know you charge interest. I know you don't support his ambitions to have his own business.

YUSUF. The sauce? I thought you would be a good influence. I campaigned for Abdelal to match you.

YASMIN. Well, thank you for your help.

YUSUF. Yasmin, I hate to say this but you will have big problems if this wedding goes ahead. The community will not stand for –

YASMIN. Sorry, Yusuf, I have to go –

YUSUF. Where?

YASMIN. The Galleries.

YUSUF. That's strange – I've just sent a car –

YASMIN *starts the engine.*

It's not... it's you? Been cutting in on our jobs. You?

YASMIN. I don't know what you're talking about.

YUSUF. Does Ashraf know about this?

YASMIN. Oh, go play with yourself, Yusuf, yes?

She hangs up.

Scene Sixteen

ASHRAF *is back in his cab, bruised and tired, still with the eye patch. His phone rings.*

JEAN. What's this about you not walking her down the aisle?

ASHRAF. Hello, ex-wife. Yes I am fine thank you so much. And you?

JEAN. I bloody mean it? What's wrong with you?

ASHRAF. It is enough that I am allowing it at all!

JEAN. She's your daughter – she loves you to bits – think how much it'd mean –

ASHRAF. No. If people find out, the community –

JEAN. Oh, for God's sake – you married me, and I'm about as Muslim as Bernard Manning drinking a pint of bloody snakebite! Do what *you* want – it doesn't matter what those extremists –

ASHRAF. They're not bloody extremists, they're devout –

JEAN. They can be all of the forty virgins rolled into one for all I care – just walk your daughter down the bloody aisle –

ASHRAF. You are not the boss of me any more!

JEAN. There were three of us in that marriage. Don't let Yusuf ruin this too.

JEAN hangs up.

ASHRAF. Bloody rude fishwife nag horse.

Scene Seventeen

The car is full of energy drinks and empty coffee cups. ASHRAF's still wearing an eye patch. He's undone quite a few buttons revealing the vest underneath his shirt. The song 'Bad Boys' by Inner Circle is on and he's singing manically.

SHAZIA and CHRIS get in the car, they look a bit alarmed. CHRIS tries to show his improvement.

CHRIS. *As-salaam alaikum*, Ashraf.

ASHRAF. You too, brother. You like reggae, man? This bit's for you, Shaz!

He sings again until:

SHAZIA. Dad! Stop!

ASHRAF. It's true though, *habibi* – you wanna let go, and I got to let you innit!

CHRIS. Ashraf, are you okay?

ASHRAF. Oh yeah, just working a lot, man – only the best for my Shazia, so got to be a pirate for a while yeah? Sailing these treachorous Wigan road-seas to bring home the booty… bounty yes?

SHAZIA. Should you really be working?

ASHRAF (*snapping*). When will you learn you do not question your father. Of course I should be bloody dogshit working.

A slightly awkward silence, ASHRAF *nods along to the beat.*

CHRIS. So what's with the reggae then, mate?

ASHRAF. A gift from one of the drug-dealers I pick up – I told him about how I used to smoke so much weed I got paranoid and he left it as a parting gift.

CHRIS. You used to smoke weed?!

ASHRAF. Course bloody not! But you got to fit in, man. Always fit in.

CHRIS. So you don't mind picking up dealers?

ASHRAF. Business is business and if you need to provide for my Shazia you better learn that quick-smart like Hussain Bolt.

It is for Allah to judge, not me. They don't bother me, I don't bother them. Simples.

A pause.

You don't like reggae?

CHRIS. I do, yeah, I love reggae.

ASHRAF. Well sing then, boy! Come on, *habibi*, you know this one!

He starts to sing 'One Love/People Get Ready' by Bob Marley & The Wailers.

Come on, you party poopers, sing!

CHRIS *and* SHAZIA *join in – reluctantly at first.*

ASHRAF *pulls over and suddenly looks incredibly tired and drawn. He scrabbles around for some paracetamol but there are none left. He pulls himself together.*

Come, let's go, Yasmin has been cooking for you all day.

SHAZIA. Just a sec, Dad.

ASHRAF. What, what is this? Yasmin will put my head in her blender if we are late. You know she's passed her citizenship test?

SHAZIA. What?! No! Oh my God, Dad. That's great news!

ASHRAF. Yes. I am stuck with her for good. How you say…
hag-ridden?! Come!

SHAZIA. Dad. She won't mind a couple of minutes. There's
something I want to ask you.

ASHRAF (*snapping*). For the love of all that is holy, Shazia,
I've told you I will do the horses but I cannot walk you down
the aisle of this heathen wedding! What will people say?

SHAZIA. I know. I wasn't going to ask that. I was just
thinking –

ASHRAF. What? What were you thinking!

SHAZIA. About all the fun times we've had in this taxi…
singing, shouting at people, laughing –

ASHRAF. You're right. It has not all been work and drug-
dealers and racist fucking English and such. This old donkey
has served us well.

SHAZIA. Exactly. And you know I'm not too sold on the horses
– I mean, what if I get kicked in the face again. You know…
I'd like you to drive me to my wedding in this. This donkey
would do me proud.

ASHRAF. You really mean this?

CHRIS. It'd be wrong to have it any other way.

ASHRAF. Okay, I will have to see if I can get back my deposit,
but you are right of course – horses are for heathens anyway.
I will shine her up, good as new, put the ribbons on there –

SHAZIA. Thanks, Dad!

*He gets some mini Union Jack flags out of his glove box and
hands them out.*

ASHRAF. You must act surprised when Yasmin breaks this
news, she will gut me like a fish if I told you first.

Scene Eighteen

ASHRAF (*now without the eye patch*) *is out of the car,*
smoking, enjoying the sunshine on his break. His phone rings,
he picks up.

YUSUF. Ashraf.

ASHRAF. Yusuf.

YUSUF. I hear it is going ahead. Shazia's marrying an infidel.

ASHRAF. Yes. She is very stubborn – I cannot change her mind.

YUSUF. This is very grave, brother. I am sorry.

ASHRAF. Yes. Me too.

YUSUF. The Koran is very clear on this: 'Believers should not
take Kafirs as friends in preference to other believers. Those
who do this will have none of Allah's protection and will
only have themselves as guards.'

ASHRAF. I have read it. Thanks.

YUSUF. Allah will no longer look over Shazia. The shame
brother! Haram!

ASHRAF. Stop. Shazia is a good Muslim girl, and Chris is a kind
man and they love each other –

YUSUF. You know that this is forbidden.

ASHRAF. What would you have me do?

YUSUF. You must disown her.

ASHRAF. I think it's time you looked to the Koran for your
own behavior. What about leaving aside what does not
concern you?

YUSUF. You are my brother, Ashraf, of course it concerns me.
I hear you are attending.

ASHRAF. I'm just driving her.

YUSUF. In the taxi? If you go through with this we will have to
call in the loan. No more taxi – we cannot be associated
with –

ASHRAF. Yusuf, listen carefully because in the words of that brilliant Muslim programme, *Allo Allo*, I will say this only once. Shazia is twice the man you will ever be and so is Chris and I'm fairly sure that Allah can work that out.

YUSUF. You know Yasmin's been driving your taxi? Your women are not in your control.

ASHRAF. Of course I know. Bloody just fuck off!

ASHRAF hangs up and lights a fag.

Scene Nineteen

SHAZIA *and* CHRIS *are waiting in the taxi. There's a bit of an atmosphere. The car radio is playing Arabic music.* SHAZIA *has henna up both her arms.*

CHRIS. He's taking his time.

SHAZIA. Probably a number two.

CHRIS. Nice.

Silence.

Look, I've said I'm sorry. I've taken it off Facebook – no one's going to see it.

SHAZIA. I know.

CHRIS. They were stupid. They just thought it would be funny.

SHAZIA. I know they did. They're fucking ignorant. I just can't understand why you didn't stop them.

CHRIS. It's my stag do. I can't just say, 'sorry guys, I can't wear a burka today because it might offend Shaz's stepmother,' can I?

SHAZIA. It's offended me! And it's not even a burka it's a fucking hijab.

CHRIS. You always used to laugh at this sort of thing. And what's all this stuff on your arm anyway?

SHAZIA. It's henna.

CHRIS. Right. Course.

SHAZIA. What?

CHRIS. Nothing!

SHAZIA. Seriously, Chris. What is it?

CHRIS. It's just.

Pause.

Well, what are you gonna wear? On the actual wedding?

SHAZIA. It's a secret, isn't it.

CHRIS. Yeah. Sure, but, just – I know you've been getting closer to your culture and that's great, but I just – well –

SHAZIA. Well what, Chris?

CHRIS. I'd just rather know, you know, if you're planning on rocking up in a burka... hijab or whatever –

SHAZIA. Right.

CHRIS. Fuck's sake.

Silence.

I'm never going to say the right thing, Shaz. I'm a blunt instrument and you know that. I just. It's all new. And I know it's a big part of you and it's important and Lord knows I love the falafel and stuff, it's just... when we met I didn't see any of that. I just saw you. And I've been brought up very... well... white. And my friends and family are even worse than me, and I guess I'm scared it's all going to be a bit well, alien, different and not what anyone expects. When all I really want to do is just marry my best friend. So...

SHAZIA. I love you, Chris. I'm wearing a white dress.

CHRIS. Cool.

SHAZIA. With a white lace niqab.

CHRIS. Right. Great, that's great.

SHAZIA. Joke! I'm joking!

CHRIS. Okay. Phew. Fuck's sake.

Scene Twenty

It's the morning of the wedding and ASHRAF *is having a fag.*
YASMIN *comes out with ribbons and a rag to polish the taxi.*
ASHRAF *stubs out the fag quickly and wafts the smoke.*

YASMIN. Ashraf.

ASHRAF. Sorry. Just… this wedding. Stress.

YASMIN. I know.

   ASHRAF *surveys the taxi.*

ASHRAF. He's been a faithful friend.

YASMIN. One last journey.

ASHRAF. He might let me keep him.

YASMIN. Don't hold your breathing eh – you will suffocate!

   Pause.

ASHRAF. We might be a bit tight for money, for a while
   anyway, until I get a job –

YASMIN. It's okay. Here.

   She hands him a wadge of cash.

ASHRAF. What is this?

YASMIN. From the, er… sewing, and my allowance. I save. It's
   time to start on Ashraf Special Sauce Facon Butties properly.
   I speak to Wigan market – they have space.

ASHRAF. That's a lot of sewing.

YASMIN. Yes. Yes it is.

ASHRAF. Thank you.

Scene Twenty-One

The cab has been decked out with ribbons and ASHRAF *is smart in a suit and tie. He waits solemnly.* SHAZIA *enters in a white gown.*

ASHRAF. *Habibi.* My *habibi.* You are beautiful.

SHAZIA. Oh, shut up, Dad, don't, you'll start me off again!

ASHRAF. No bridesmaids?

SHAZIA. They're at the venue. I thought it'd be nice for you and me to have some time.

Pause.

It looks awesome, Dad.

ASHRAF. Yes – well it seems Yasmin was doing some moonlighting!

SHAZIA. Er –

ASHRAF. Sewing apparently. It's fine… turns out we're all as crazy as each other. Come.

They get in the cab.

SHAZIA. What's that smell?

ASHRAF. Ashraf's Special Sauce Pie Balls – for the guests.

SHAZIA. Great.

She takes the Joop and starts to spray it to cover the smell.

Go on then, crank up the tunes! And put your foot down – Chris hates it when I'm late.

ASHRAF. That bloody cow-licker can wait. He's the luckiest man on God's earth.

SHAZIA. Music please, Dad! And his name is Chris!

ASHRAF *puts on* SHAZIA'*s favourite Arabic tune 'I'm Not a Heathen' and cranks it up.*

ASHRAF. You know you can still change your mind? Omar still wanting a wife for his nephew.

SHAZIA. Thanks for that, Dad – it's good to have a back-up plan, but I've sort of made my mind up now.

ASHRAF. Well, you know the prophet said that when you get married you have completed half of your religion. So I guess half is better than none!

SHAZIA. Exactly – and to be fair, I'm only half Muslim.

ASHRAF. She would've converted if I'd asked her.

SHAZIA. Ha!

ASHRAF. And that veil is almost a hijab.

SHAZIA. It's all for you, Dad!

They sing along for a bit. ASHRAF *pulls over.*

ASHRAF. I've got something for you.

SHAZIA. You shouldn't have – you can't aff–

ASHRAF. Shut up, woman! I am your father – respect at all times! It's for your customs. Something 'old'.

ASHRAF *unchains a thin chain from around his neck, on it is a ring.*

SHAZIA. What is it?

ASHRAF. It's my wedding ring. To your mother. I hope it brings you luck.

SHAZIA *pulls a face – their marriage ended in divorce!*

I mean it, *habibi*! We were very happy, we just made some mistakes. I listened to the wrong people, no flexible. I wasn't as wise as you, but we loved each other very much.

He puts the necklace on her.

And if you can't bloody embrace Islam then why don't you bloody embrace Wigan? Your mother made the best Yorkshire puddings I have ever tasted. All you've ever made me is Pot Noodle Chicken and Mushroom! Some bloody wife you'll be!

SHAZIA. Dad! Language! (*Pause.*) Any more nuggets of wisdom before I go in?

ASHRAF. Yes. Don't be a jacket potato.

SHAZIA. Er what?

ASHRAF. You heard! Don't be like jacket potato. Sitting around watching Jeremy Kyle all day. Not good for marriage or career.

SHAZIA. I think you mean couch potato, Dad. You know, on the couch?

ASHRAF. Whatever, work hard, at everything. That's my wisdom for you.

SHAZIA. Thanks.

ASHRAF. Are you okay?

SHAZIA. Bit scared I guess.

ASHRAF. It's okay, *habibi*. I'll be with you all the way.

SHAZIA. You're walking me?

ASHRAF. Bloody course I am – I need to look that cow-licker Kevin in the eye when I give you away. So he knows what's bloody coming to him if he ever steps out of the line. Not that you are my possession to give him, of course. You are independent woman just like Beyoncé.

SHAZIA *bursts into tears*.

Don't cry! I joke. I know his name is Chris.

Silence.

SHAZIA. Right. I'm ready.

ASHRAF. Let's go then!

They get out of the car. SHAZIA *takes his arm. He pats the car in a silent goodbye. They walk round the car to the front of the space.*

(*Singing under his breath*.) HERE COMES THE BRIDE, ALL FAT AND WIDE!

SHAZIA *elbows him in the ribs. The cab fades away. Big smiles, the flash of a camera. The music kicks in. Lights.*

The End.

WIND BIT BITTER, BIT BIT BIT HER

Sami Ibrahim

Wind Bit Bitter, Bit Bit Bit Her was first performed at VAULT Festival, London, on 24 January 2018, with the following cast:

MARY   Phoebe Vigor
CHARLEY   Rosa Coduri

Director   Sami Ibrahim
Lighting   Jack Taylor
Music   David Ridley
Poster Design   Laura Whitehouse

Characters

MARY
CHARLEY

Note on Play

Text should be spoken at a frantic pace

(except when it shouldn't).

A dash on its own line – is either a pause, or a moment when a character can't or won't speak.

ONE

MARY, *Dymchurch, England, 2020s*.

Mary.
Spelt like normal.
And then, uh, it's Malek, my surname.
M-A-L-E-K
But I thought you'd have that down already, or –
Just to check, right.
Her as well?
I really thought you'd have this down somewhere, you've met her, you've –
Again, just to check.
Sure, for the record, or something.
Sorry.
I'm a bit –
Her, yeah.
She's Charley.
Dimmock.
She's not my girlfriend though, she's –
Uh
D-I-M... M –
Yeah, exactly.
If you ever saw *Ground Force*, like the ginger one –
Yeah.
Charley's spelt differently though.
E-Y, yeah – no, not a nickname.
–
Just put teacher – reception.
And stop saying girlfriend.
Please.
If you'd.
Again.
With the girlfriend.
Um.
She's a teacher too.

But secondary, not –
Excuse me.
Sorry.
Can we –
Can you please stop calling her a girlfriend, cos she's not my
girlfriend, we're married, we're –
Um.
Sorry?
Proof of what?
No.
No.
I'm not hearing this.
I don't understand why you need proof, if there's a next of kin
it's me, we signed a thing when we got in and I don't –
If you've lost it then –
This shitting hospital is –
I am calm.
Is that clear?
I'm calm.
And don't tell me to...
–
I'm the mum, okay? You speak to me.
So he speaks to me.
The doctor from St Saviour's Hospital explains what's
happened, takes me through the complications like a shopping
list.
Charley
Twenty-six weeks
Seizure
A&E
Pre-Eclampsia
High blood pressure
which I already know.
But then there's
Risk of suffocation
Risk of death
Caesarean
Early delivery
and after that there's
Underdeveloped lungs
Ventilator support

Scarring
Failing lungs
Failed lungs
And that means

–

And they double-check spelling cos it needs to be registered.
Which is great, really good to know it will go down in a
register, that someone even makes a register, and keeps it up to
date, and gathers all the informations on every birth, except it's
not a birth, it's the opposite – proof in writing that nothing
happened.
Good to get a head-start on the bureaucracy.
Then the doctor clutches my hand and looks at me, square, and
gives me a smile so pathetic it makes me sick, like he wants to
prostrate himself and moan it'll all be okay, Ms Malek, I
promise, it will be.
But he doesn't.
Instead, he asks if we named her.
Which we didn't.
Or we didn't out loud.
Or maybe Charley did in her head.
Or at least I did:
Miriam.
My daughter Miriam, because I'm a Mary, and a Miriam is a
little Mary – but I'm too embarrassed to say it, cos the doctor's
looking at me so intently, so sad, and I can't spoil that, can't
make him think I'm such a desperate mummy, not worthy of his
big sad eyes.
But there it is: Miriam.
Miriam hovering on my tongue's tip.
Miriam she was, is, would be, she should be. And look at us:
I imagine giving her big squish-hugs, turning us into Play-Doh,
mashed together in a Play-Doh goo, and you can't separate out
Play-Doh, not perfectly: always bits of Mary-dough hidden in
Miriam-dough and Miriam-dough hidden in Mary-dough so
might as well leave us alone in one big mass.
Mi-ri-am
The syllables linger, three of them, I'm trying to push them out
my mouth.

–

Nothing comes – like a vacuum cleaner's sucking syllables

back down my throat.
Same vacuum that sucked the air out of Miriam.
And it's whirring loud, louder.
It is LOUD.
I think of Play-Doh, of bright colours, of squishing, of Miriam,
of anything and
it feels like I'm gone for days – I snap back to the room.
Did you want to name the child?
And he is ever so patient, the most patient human on the planet.
Did you want to name the child, Ms Malek?
No.
No, thank you, kindly.
No.
I don't know if I can't or I won't.
I decide it's cos I won't.
I'm not bringing myself to share, not with him, none of his
business, Miriam's name.
He smiles,
not to worry,
and scribbles onto a pink form and looks up at me, smiling his
calm, considerate smiling smile.
I mutter something so soft I can't understand.
Excuse me?
If it's possible.
If it's no trouble.
I ask if I can see Miriam.
–
–
–
–

TWO

He hesitates and then relents and now we're passing through
wards.
6 a.m.
I'm trailing his steps, through doors, through wards
First – stuffed with old people
Second – sadder old people
Third – foreign old people
And my mind's wondering over decisions, Charley's decision,
she made a decision.
No: be fair: the doctors told her to make the decision: she had to
make the decision because there was a threat to her life.
Her. Life.
Capital L.
And that's a line crossed – where Charley stops making
sacrifices and starts looking after number one, and Miriam's
removed and we're left with –
Her decision and –
It's a horrible thing to think, cos we're defined by our decisions
and if that's Charley's decision then –
it's horrible to think.
Cos maybe I would've made a different decision.
Or maybe not.
But it's never a competition.
And then the doctor stops: we're here.
The arse-end of the hospital, a cramped room, a miniature Lego
model morgue.
They said private trusts would be better, but this is miserable.
Needs cleaning, needs better interior design.
The doctor coughs a little, slight – and I notice his hand, stuck
out, willing me to look.
–
There it is, lying, on a slat, cold, but not freezing, a lump
covered by a sheet of white.
I think it's my lump.
I know it's my lump cos the doctor's still gesturing to it, with
his soft gesture, soft hands, directing my eyes – but my eyes
can't follow through,
can't bring themselves to –
and they flick beyond my lump, distract themselves with the
rest of the room.

And they notice rows of these lumps.
A Play-Doh factory.
Row on row.
Too many of them – one is too many, but dozens is sickening,
and they're all covered with the same soft white fabric.
My vision shifts focus, in, out over that fabric – it's cheap,
disposable, barely a tissue, and the contours give away tiny
noses,
or folded knees,
a chin,
a bloated belly,
a foot, a left foot – three rows down, last on the left.
Should be covered, but it's not, it sticks out, it's liquid, it's
floating, pale, paler more stripped of life than anything real.
I tense my throat, try to shut my gullet off from vomit.
But the doctor, he notices, he's noticing the hunched shoulders
and my clenched throat, so he puts his hand to my back and
tells me perhaps it's best if we leave.
He's having a hard time of it.
Poor guy.
I'm not moving.
And he can feel my back stiffen.
So he tries again, a bit more forceful, but never anything less
than over-the-top-back-bending niceness.
I shuffle a step but –
The uncovered foot twitches.
I swear it.
Mary looks down at it, pauses, her body contracts.
The doctor attempts eye contact with Mary but fails.
Mary stares at the foot until, again, it twitches: a small, subtle
twitch.
The doctor tilts his head.
Ms Malek?
Mary?
And I turn back to him – like I'm accusing him, and for a
second, I swear the doctor thinks I know something I shouldn't,
thinks I've seen something I shouldn't
but my mind is gone, I know nothing, I know no things
and that twitch,
which I swear I saw but I swear never happened,
gnaws at my head.

Mary looks back at the foot.
I'm blinking, trying to figure out if I can trust my eyes.
And I try to stammer out a sentence,
something
I can't figure out what I'm saying,
something
my brain's not connecting to my mouth to my ears, and
something
close to:
did-that-foot-or-am-I-surely-not-I-think-I-might-sitting-down-
would-be-*twitching*?
–

The look I get back is one of absolute sympathy.
He's not answering my question, he's just looking at me.
And then the doctor's hands reach out and he sweeps me up, out
the room away from questions about twitches and itchy feet,
quicker than I can manage
and I realise I haven't even looked at my lump
MY lump,
still there,
lifeless,
or maybe twitching
but before I'm through the door I take one last look
and see if maybe it's moving and
I think perhaps I see
SOMETHING
under the white fabric
a breath a jerk a hand waving
maybe
a mouth crying
it's screaming don't leave
or maybe –
is that –
maybe
a spasm, a twitch
or –
maybe
or –
but the doctor
and –
and I'm –

–

I'm out in the corridor,

–

not quite processing.

–

The doctor squeezes my shoulders, smiles, says my brain needs
a rest.

–

Charley's in recovery, she's resting, and I should rest too.
This is difficult, this is very very difficult.
I am assured it will be fine, the doctor assures me.
I will collect Charley, we will drive home, we will support each
other, we will be fine.
I smile at him.
Nice man.
A really nice man.
A really nice man who assures me nothing's wrong with his big
eyes.
But in that moment I decide something is wrong.
I decide I saw Miriam twitch because I trust my own eyes,
I trust them and I
breathe out.

–

–

–

–

THREE

Car window's shut, we're sat in a vacuum.
11 a.m.
Mary drives, Charley sits next to her.
We've spoken exactly two words.
I know.
I hugged her, her eyes oozed, and I said
I know.
That's all.
And she just nodded.
That was in the ward, then I wheeled her to the car and she
remained wordless, like she believes, in this car, silence is
enough.
Like we don't need to talk things through – and I can't be
bothered with it.
You know?
Fuck it,
I'm not doing silence,
it's not a time for silence.
–
–
–

Charley dominates.
If she says we don't talk, we don't talk, and that's that.
–
–

Could tell her about Miriam.
She'd think I'm nuts.
–
–

Or could put on the radio, have some noise, so I reach over –
Travel and weather – Storm Edgar – whipping by – and
DON'T.
Please.
–
–

Fine.
–

Not sure if this is healthy.
I know this isn't healthy.
We should be talking – I have words, I want them out in the

open and I need to get them out there cos otherwise they'll rot
me from inside.
–

But she's not letting me.
Or: worse, she's got none.
Which is painful to think.
She can't find words.
Lacking in words,
opinions
thoughts,
cowardice, basically, scared to admit that there *are* words and
too thick to find them.
Cos there are always words.
Might be nonsense, might be empty, might be hurtful,
but they're there.
Jumbled up, up there,
just gotta get them out,
get the lid off,
catharsis,
hammer to the head,
balls to the wall,
clit to the wall,
fucking
JABBER
JABBER
JABBER
No.
–

The pair sit in silence.
My words bubble up.
Her words all flat.
But it's never a competition.
–

–

–

–

FOUR

I'm eyeing her.
3 p.m.
On the sofa, now, she's lying, affected, damp cloth over her
face, like the mourning process is a luxury spa.
You alright?
–

Nothing.
A nod.
Was that a nod?
So small I barely trust my eyes.
–

You alright Chaz?
I've never called her Chaz before.
Why would I call her Chaz?
And she sits up,
she removes the cloth, painfully, and lets her gaze nestle into
me.
It's part *leave me alone*
part *why d'you call me that?*
I know in an instant she hates it.
That's obvious – there's nothing here to like and me calling her
Chaz has tipped something in her brain and I can feel her
erupting.
Her mouth twitches –
–

Still nothing.
Then: a nod.
Then: I'll pass.
–

I'll pass – she says.
Brilliant.
Breaking news.
Then the cloth is draped back over her eyes.
And she is serene – her towelette is baby-blue and it's typical,
by the way, I remind myself this, cos I can't forget it, it's typical
that Charley has to be a saint,
has to mourn like a woman anointed.
And I have to be manic.
That's our balance.
Always is.

But not this time.
Not when we're
tilted.

–

So I'll cheer her up, wheel out an old joke:

Bitter bitter Charley, old weary grump,
Sitting all alone, and giving me the hump.

She's not thrilled with that, so I try –
Place is dirty, Charley – shall I give it a clean, get the vacuum
out…?
Nope, try again.
New curtains, what d'you think?
Nothing: the baby, then, Charley, let's talk that through, yeah,
shall we do that?

–

And I let it hang over her.
Maybe the gust of that word – baby – can blow the flannel off
her face.
Or maybe the clouds outside'll do it.

–

Yeah?
Shall we do that?
Talk about the –
About *it*?

–

I can't say *baby* again.
Once was fine – just about.
And I could say Miriam.
But then I'd have to explain Miriam.
So I let *it* be the word I use.

–

It.
Let it drip down onto her – rouse her.

–

The windows are shaking.
Just a bit – not lots, but enough.
It adds tension.
So as her blindfold slips off and her eyes jut up at me I almost
can't hold myself steady.
But I do.

I make sure to.
Rock-steady.
And the windows are shaking but I'm not moving.
Storm Edgar's outside – he is screaming and violent; we are
silent and violent.
For a moment.
Rock-steady vs. rock-steady.
Swelling.
Ready to burst.
Windows shaking.
Beating.
And a word forms on Charley's bottom lip.
Fury arriving.
I feel it.
And I'm puffed up.
And her lip moves.
Words forming.
Windows drum harder.
Mary pricks.
Charley stalks.
Mouths twitching.
Arguments we ache for.
Words to be hurled.
Beating.
Drumming.
A deluge from her mouth and curses in mine.
And we buckle in.
Her lip quaking.
We buckle in.
Brewing.
Beating.
Louder.
Rumbling.
Louder.
BURSTING.
–
Then she wobbles.
That's all: her bottom lip wobbles.
No words, just –
Charley droops back down onto the sofa.
Her back flops.

The windows tremble and amongst the vibrations there's
a sobbing.
Takes me a moment to locate it: Charley's crying hard.
So hard it doesn't come out, it implodes inside her.
I need to hug her, it hurts watching her and I need to hug her.
But for the first time in fifteen years I'm not sure how.
She's huddled over, her is voice is muffled – the sound of crying
is a fox's wail.
And I stand over her.
I hover.
I feel stupid.
I feel awkward.
So I sit because it's less awkward.
Pause a moment.
Watch her.
Ease in next to her.
Slow,
no room for sudden movement.
I clutch her hand.
I swear I feel a flinch or a twitch, but it's nothing, it's nerves,
because she takes my hand and places it right there in the folds
of her body and squeezes.
Her body squeezes.
And we're completely safe, so we pause time in that position,
for as long as we can,
cos it's perfect.
–
Mary starts to fidget.
She looks over to Charley, smiles.
You holding up?
Mary smiles again – lets her buck teeth show.
No response.
We should talk.
No response.
Mary wriggles out from Charley's grip.
We should, Charley.
No response.
Mary stands.
Charley stays seated, looks up at Mary, blank.
And I glare back down at her.
Well?

I'll pass, M.
It's all that flicks between us.
I'll pass.
–

It's a stupid joke we have – cos we're teachers.
And it's not appropriate. Not now.
Wrong words, wrong time.
I don't say it but I make my eyes transmit it, like she has to
know I'm fuming cos she said *I'll pass* when I want an honest
answer.
And her look back says *I don't care* and I believe her.
I do,
in that moment,
I really believe she doesn't care.
So it's ten seconds I give her,
in my head,
that's my limit.
One last chance.
I've decided it, right now, five seconds
till I'm breathing air,
storming out.
Three
Two
–

Mary turns around, walks to the door.
From behind, Charley calls.
M?
M?!
But I'm not breaking, I'm done, I'm out.
–
–
–
–

FIVE

The sea's wild.
5 p.m.
Water flopping onto the shore and it's bracing, it's fucking
freezing too, but I need it, so I stand and watch, out, past the
waves and let Storm Edgar whip me.
It's a slap, stinging, a THWACK to the face, wakes me.
Ice up my nostrils, like my body's sucking in a swirl of air.
And it's chilling me, air racing up and down my figure, pulsing
through me, stretches, moulds, my body, eclipses all the things
that should be blinding me right now.
And it means I can breathe – deep.
And watch the waves as they smack me, the rain as it –
Mary looks down.
Ice hurling itself at me.
Mary notices something.
–

It's a foot.
–

A child's, a left foot,
but it's disconnected from any body.
It's afloat.
–

Hacked off with a knife.
I think.
It's bobbing in front of me but my eyes can't settle on it for the
rain.
But it's real.
That's what my eyes tell me:
it's a real, dismembered, foot.
–

And I know it's real cos it looks fake.
Pure and clean, like a porcelain doll, foot snapped off, scrubbed
and placed on the beach half a mile from my house for me to find.
–

Attached to a toe, the big one, there's a tag, thin piece of card,
writing scrawled on, ink faded, washed out.
I think it says *St Saviour's*.
Which makes sense cos it looks like the foot I saw twitch.
Mary looks around – no one.
She's an alien on an empty rut of land.

And that foot's the closest thing to something human.
I want it.
I want to own the foot.
I feel in my coat pocket: there's a Tesco bag for life – and
I think, perhaps, it might be the perfect home for that foot.
I take out the bag, eye up the foot.
Mary picks it up.
She's gone.
–
–
–
–

SIX

Music.
6 p.m.
Pulsing out windows and Mary stands solid, listening.
She's at the end of the garden, notes wind down the garden path
– soft at first, then louder, louder until –
I hear a bass line
throbbing
POUND
into my ear
and it's driving
warring drums.
Charley's voice, inside, her voice is tone-deaf.
Scratching into my ear.
Mary approaches the front door, swings it open, steps inside and
Charley emerges from the next room, pushing up to me, with a
face contorted: sadder than I've ever seen it, happier than I've
ever seen it.
She comes to hug me, launches herself onto me, she smells
moist – like her tears are damp, rising.
And I stay stiff, let her hug it out, her breath over me, closing in
on my ear, snuggling in, and her singing stops.
It's replaced by a soft voice – wobbling.
I'm sorry, M.

I'm sorry.

She says it like she knows what she's apologising for.

And she hasn't bothered to ask if I'm alright – I've gone out in the middle of a storm and she's forgotten to ask if I'm alright.

I'm sorry, M.

Drips out her mouth.

I've been a miserable shit...

We're all miserable shits, Charley, that's the way it is, and if you think you've got to apologise for it, you've missed the point.

I don't say that.

I smile at her, meek, I think it's passive-aggressive – but apparently it's smiley enough that Charley sees acceptance.

And she grabs my hands, lifts them up, gets me to dance.

She did this at our wedding.

She always misjudges.

I think, for a moment, she's genuinely happy.

But I'm bitter, I'm boiling – my coat's still on, the heating's full blast and in my right pocket: the foot, weighing me down, heavy as a fucking really heavy brick.

It's a black hole, sucking everything in.

I'm leaning off to the right, the foot's dragging me to the floor, and Charley thinks I'm just trying to get out of dancing, so she goes

NO NO NO NO NO –

Up I come,

back to the dance,

and I'm trying to wriggle out from her grip, it's hot, the coat is hot and heavy, and Charley sees me sweating, sees me uncomfortable, sees me leaning, blithering, so she does the one thing she thinks will help.

And I see it coming – a flash in her eyes, a twinge in her body, she grinds up on me.

She always misjudges.

Charley pulls Mary close to her, slobbers into Mary's ear.

There are so many ways to fold you up round my tongue –

I wanna go through them all.

The music cuts.

And I feel sick.

–

I tell her I need to get changed first.

Then, head down, into the kitchen, right hand in my right pocket, fiddling.

Charley hasn't turned off the stereo.
THUMP
after
THUMP
continues, and I'm in front of the freezer, figuring that it's
probably better to freeze this foot than let it rot in my pocket.
There's a bag of carrots, some chips, ice cream, more chips, and
an old veggie lasagne – except we gave up rabbit food a decade
ago.
And then, behind that, some peas.
My hand's still in my pocket, fiddling with the bag – and inside
that bag, that lump, of squidgy fat bones.
Mary pulls it out her pocket.
Mary opens up the bag, peers inside.
It's almost fluorescent, I see a halo around it.
I let the freezer air spike my face.
One track comes to an end in the other room – I'm bracing
myself for what comes next.
–
I'm thrown off, turn back to see what's going on, the bag slips
out my hand onto the floor, and in that moment –
M?
What are you up to?
You upstairs?
Shit.
–
Frozen.
Shit.
Uh.
Yeah?
You in the kitchen?
–
–
No.
–
Silence hangs and, quiet, I hear footsteps, Charley's getting
closer, I hear her stumble.
M?
Then my mind snaps back and I grab the bag, blue and red
squiggles that make up the word Tesco, stuff it in the freezer
behind the peas.
Charley's at the kitchen door.

I slam the freezer door.
And I face away from her.

–

What are you up to, M?
Still face away from her.
M?

–

Then turn.
Big smile.
Happy face.

–

Hey.
Just –
What's going on?

–

Charley's question; Mary remains silent.

–

I'm just putting a child's foot in the freezer, Charley, that's all.
I reckon I shouldn't say that...
I mutter something about looking for a snack.
Ice cream, I want ice cream.
Choc-chip.
And her look is opaque: so you don't want to, you know, do *stuff*?
She mutters this, I think she's disappointed, or maybe relieved
we don't have to bother fucking.
It wouldn't have been worth it.
I just sort of twitch my head – non-committal.
I think she's about to leave,
but she doesn't, she takes a step forward.
She asks me where the ice cream is – if I want ice cream, why
haven't I taken it out?
I'm flicking through excuses, none of them sticking, all flushing
through me.
I can't shake the thing I want to explain to her.
Maybe I should just say it, something's up, Charley, maybe
Miriam's alive, there's some massive sci-fi conspiracy down the
hospital, we should team up, fucking sort it –
But I know she won't listen, cos instead she's great at telling me
to calm down.
So I want to push all these thoughts down.
Get them out my brain, but there's nothing else in my brain.

So I give into it.
–
Deep breath.
Let Charley know the words in my head.
–
I say it.
–
And I'm looking for a reaction.
But it's like the sentence hasn't even reached Charley's ears,
she just stares back at me.
Then she comes close, draws me in for a hug.
Squeeeeezes.
Oh, M, M, you need sleep like nothing I've seen.
She's right.
And I smile, nestle into her.
It feels safe.
–
You don't really believe that, do you, M?
–
And tell her I don't.
I'm tired, I'm tired and I know our child is gone, I know that,
I just need sleep is all.
Sometimes my brain –
Sleep'll straighten me out.
I smile and
I tell her that.
–
–
–
–

SEVEN

I'm on three hours' sleep – sort of: two were spent staring at the back of Charley's head.

4 a.m.

She's going grey.

Probably not worth mentioning that now.

Mary sits in the kitchen, clutches onto an embroidery hoop.

It calms her – we see, with every stitch, the tension falling from her body.

The pattern is intricate, abstract, colourful.

–

She closes her eyes, breathes out.

–

And opens up.

We haven't spoken, again, we do things in silence.

She brushed her teeth – I didn't bother – then she went straight to bed.

Not even a *goodnight*.

Or a cuddle.

She got off to sleep – I couldn't.

Can't sleep at a time like this – I need calm.

And 3:53 a.m. is as calm as it gets – even Storm Edgar's asleep.

–

Another stitch.

And another.

Mary's keeps sewing, slow at first, then faster and faster, until she stabs her index finger with the needle.

Shit.

Ow.

OWW FUCK!

Mary sucks her finger.

Mary pulls it out her mouth, examines it.

–

From above: footsteps.

Mary stops examining her finger, looks up to the ceiling.

Shit.

She's up.

Fuck's sake.

I didn't ask for company.

She'll come in here, I know it, course she will, she's going to come in here and will interrupt and –

–
Then I can't hear the steps.
Has she gone back to bed or –
The TV blares from the other room.
There it is – noise spewing out.
And it's much louder than silence.
–
She knows I'm in here.
She doesn't want to speak to me, but she wants her presence
KNOWN, so she turns on the telly to make sure I KNOW, know
she's going nowhere.
Mary tries to sew, tries to ignore the sound,
one stitch
two stitch
then gives up.
Mary's finger taps.
–
Then, from the other room:
M?
YOU SEEN THIS?
I'll give it a second, make her think I haven't heard.
M?!
YOU SEEN THIS?
No, course I haven't seen it, cos I'm not watching the telly, am
I?
M?!
Right, I'm going upstairs.
–
But Charley stops me.
She catches me as I'm going up, says it's terrible, says I have to
come see.
So here I stand.
Charley's next to me, eyes wide open, glazed over with tears.
Not crying for the thing she should be crying about but crying
over the news.
And I cannot summon the energy to comfort her.
It's dull.
Some report about kids abandoned at birth – some family that
can't afford third-child costs.
Charley grabs onto my arm – too tight, fingers dug in.
And I stare at her grip.
Then one report ends, and another starts up.

Charley goes to turn off the telly, I tell her to leave it.
There's reporter, on a beach, on the south coast, battered by wind.
Limbs – is what she's talking about.
Washed up on the sand, she says, dozens of sightings of
washed-up body parts.
And no one can account for it.
And the police are trawling through unsolved murders, missing
person cases.
But they're coming up short.
And anyone with information should step forward...
I have information.
Maybe I should step forward.
Charley lets go – but then she starts speaking, so it's like she's
just gripping me tighter.
Charley's mouth whirring.
Maybe I should step forward – but it's my information, not to
share, it's mine.
Head straight.
Ignore her, think.
Charley asks me to think about it.
I'm trying to think, I'm trying to –
But I realise we're not thinking about the same thing.
Just think about it – she blurts it out again.
About what?
Maybe we should move on...
What's she saying?
Maybe this
Maybe that
She keeps talking
I'm barely listening What is it?
Won't take long
healthy
a step forward
progress
What?
WHAT IS?
I look at her.
What are you saying?
You're not listening. She mumbles – she's taking offence.
And I go quiet.
She tilts her head
and says we should try adoption.

–
–
–
–

EIGHT

Breakfast is coffee.
5 a.m.
We *share* a pot, so that's something.
But before our mugs are drained, I feel it coming.
There it is, a name, perfectly round and plump, it forms on
Charley's lips and she pushes it into the stagnant air between us
– like it has a right to be there.
Eleanor.
I look at her – she's serious.
Nadine.
More serious than she should be.
Alia.
Shit.
She wants to adopt a child and name it.
Malika.
She wants to go through it all again.
Jane.
My head's getting –
Gemma
And the sky has taken my side – it looks furious.
Hannah
Ready to erupt.
Dina
But I stay calm.
Nadia
I am polite.
Maya
But Charley builds a rhythm.
Fiona
Lara
Each name a beat against my head.
Yasmin

Sophie
Mary smacks the table, with each name an open-palmed
bang
Charlotte
bang
Rita
bang
Alex
bang
Sara
bang
we see fury building, each
bang
like another ratchet
bang
like something sparks her on
bang
cos I can feel it
bang
that each name
bang
Jessica
bang
Margot
bang
is proof
bang
bang
sorry, M
bang
are you not?
bang
cos I am!
bang
I'm fine!
bang
Ellen
bang
Charlotte
bang
Rose

bang
I've mourned and moved on
bang
like a psycho
bang
like a psycho
bang
pick a name
bang
MARY
bang
PICK A NAME
bang
Josie
bang
Maddy
bang
Beth
bang
MARY
BANG
and the only name I have screaming in my head is Miriam but
she'll never know it and I'll never say it so I sit silent and nod at
the names as they hit:
VICTORINANCYJULIPHOEBAGATHANNANTONIRISSAL
LEMILALICIAVANESSA

–

–

Charley stops.
She says she's heard something in the other room, I say it's
nothing but she's –
SHH.

–

We listen.
Just the wind, the sound of thin glass vibrating – but what do
you expect, there's a storm out.
Charley widens her eyes at me, she juts a finger up in the air – it
demands silence, like my thoughts are clouding her ears.
Christ, it's nothing, it's just –
But she's off, into the TV room, like she's bored.
I stay at the table.

–

This is pissing me off.

If we're gonna do this, then let's do it.

She doesn't get to start a conversation then abandon it, leave me
in the lurch, leave –

CHARLEY?!

–

Fuck's sake.

CHARLEY, CAN WE –

I'm brought short by a scream.

Mary stands.

Then a crash, like the house is collapsing, then another scream,
monstrous, then another, louder, higher, and the sound of fury
blasting into the house.

–

–

Charley's face is cut up.

Not badly, just a bit, a shard of glass caught her face.

So I'm trying to comfort her: plaster, wet towel, dabbing the
cut, and she's giving me a look that says she doesn't want me
patronising her.

I tell her I'm matronising her.

She doesn't laugh.

She's fiddling with her phone, she wants to call the fire brigade
– I tell her there's no point.

Storm's been going all night and we're not the only house with
a tree through their window.

We gotta wait it out.

But she calls anyway.

–

Then she hangs up.

Well?

She couldn't get through.

So we stand in a fuming silence.

I keep trying to clean up her cut, but she shakes me off.

Fine.

Let it get infected.

Charley turns to me.

Go for a walk?

And we're off.

–

–
–
–

NINE

There's this frown on Charley's face and it's deep.
7 a.m.
We're trudging.
The beach is empty, apart from, right on the edge of the ocean,
a cluster of people.
We're walking towards them, but Charley doesn't notice.
We keep trudging.
I'm waiting for that crowd to split, but it doesn't, it stays tight –
the circle is silent.
Charley finally notices.
She looks up ahead, asks what I think it's for, but I shrug.
And it's like Charley's irritated cos I don't have an answer for
her, so she pushes up ahead, rushes even, and dissolves into the
crowd.
She's a kid, whose nose needs to be stuck into everything all
at once.
I slow my walk down, I'm not nosy, I'll get there when I get
there, no rush.
Mary slows to a halt.
Mary looks ahead, she pauses.
Then Mary paces forward, quick, barging her way through the
crowd.
The circle is stunned,
vacuumed empty.
Charley's opposite me.
Our eyes connect for half a second,
then drop down
to the sand.
A hand and half a forearm.
Cut off.
Just like before:
pale, tiny and porcelain.

It floats.
And there's a flash of green which draws my eye – right in the
middle of the limb, embedded, it's –
Seaweed, maybe, or grass, but no –
It looks unnatural, plastic.
The fuck is it?
I want to reach out and grab it, find out out where the green's
come from, find out if there's a hospital tag, if –
But I can't.
Too many people.
Too much fear to twitch.
So I wait.
They'll disperse eventually.
I wait.
And I focus on the hand.
–

One person leaves.
Then two more – they start a trend – then Charley comes over.
She grabs my shoulder.
Let's get back, M – but I'm barely registering her.
I'm feeling my brain getting wound up.
This is private, I don't want people, I want myself, alone.
Charley shakes me again,
and I rip myself from under her, stare at her.
WHAT?
No response.
What?
She can't be bothered to answer.
I'm staying, I tell her, go back, I'll follow.
Now she's pissed:
whining about having to sort out the window by herself,
moaning about being cold, like it's my fault she forgot to bring
a coat.
I tell her: go home then.
And it slams her, heavy, heavy enough that she crumples.
Charley hovers, next to me, for a while, and I wonder when
she'll pluck up the courage to just piss off.
I think she's trying to make eye contact, but I stare down.
And Charley gives in.
She leaves and others follow – they disperse in waves, until I am,
finally, alone.

–
There's no hospital tag – it probably washed off.
But the flash of green is a wire.
There's the stub of an arm, with a thin green wire embedded in
it – acrylic green plastic coating stretched copper, with its
frayed metal lines stretching out the plastic out the flesh.
I tug at it.
It's stuck in there.
I flip the limb over and see a thin, barely perceptible dotted line:
stitches, stretching down the centre of the wrist – where the
skin's been pulled apart and sewn back together.
Mary weighs the limb in her hand.
Her eyes drift over it.
This is mad.
–

But my mind can't stop fiddling, my hand can't stop fiddling.
Mary reaches for the wire again, pulls at it.
Enough pressure and I can feel it dislodge, it's coming loose.
Mary pulls harder, twists it
and the wire bursts out, the force jerks my arm, and the limb
vomits up its innards.
There's bone sticking out, deposits of fat, blood blotting onto
the sand, stringy tears of muscle, and amongst it all is the green
wire.
Which connects, right at the end, to a little cuboid of gold.
And on the cuboid is a little diamond logo – barely visible, but
I examine it from every angle and see the gold glisten and blink
and feel a drip on my face.
Feels like a tear,
dripping down my cheek,
so I go to wipe it off, check my hand and see a dirt-red stain.
From the limb.
Must've splattered.
Mary wipes her face with her sleeve.
Oh shit.
That's horrible.
That's stale, a rust-iron taste in my mouth.
Mary gags.
I need water.
Or gum, or –
It's making me –

Mary drops the limb.
She rushes forward, wades in the sea, falls onto her knees.
Mary cups her hands, fills them with seawater.
Better than this.
Anything is.
Mary gulps it down.
Mary gags.
–

The seawater drowns out the taste for
Two seconds
Three seconds
Then it's back.
A fist strangling me from inside.
No breath left.
A wave closing in.
Smashing onto her and Mary scrambles backwards.
On hands and knees.
Mary bends down, places her forehead on the sand, breathes in
deep.
Her breath rasping.
Make it better
The limb is right in front of me now.
Gooey, red.
And the wire right next to it, that diamond logo flashing – it
knows something I want to know
Mary staggers to her feet.
Mary fishes into her pocket, pulls out a plastic bag.
Sainsbury's this time – bag for life.
Mary picks up the limb, drops it inside the bag.
Mary picks up the wire, plunges it into her pocket, walks off.
–
–
–
–

TEN

Mary?

8 a.m.

Step through the front door and there's a bag.

It's packed.

And I know what's happened – immediately, I know.

Charley's found the foot.

Her bag's by the door, packed tight so it won't zip up, and her toothbrush is sticking out the top like a plastic purple middle finger.

She's leaving.

She's trying to get out before I come home.

She's sneaky.

And I'm not built to handle her.

And it's cowardly, taking off without words, she's –

My head blurs.

I don't need this.

Mary's bent double.

I don't need this, Charley, I need a hug.

Then Mary's up, straight.

Mary storms through to the kitchen.

Charley's seen it, seen a foot, frozen solid in the freezer, and is terrified of who her wife is and she wants out and

and I don't blame her.

Mary opens the freezer, throws it wide.

I'd want out if this was –

But it's still there, hidden, behind the peas.

Is that relief?

Should I be feeling relief?

Charley hasn't found it.

I don't think.

It hasn't moved, still right where it was.

CHARLEY?

No response.

This is relief.

I'm starting to feel relief.

I've misread things, it's not what I think, it's –

Mary crams the new limb in and slams the freezer door.

Charley hasn't found anything, and maybe I'm confused, and maybe Charley's not leaving.

She's not leaving, Charley's –

And maybe I just need sleep.
Calm me –
Calm my head down.
And maybe I've jumped to conclusions, and –
Fuck, I'm an idiot when I –

CHARLEY. Mary?

MARY. all in my head.

CHARLEY. Mary?

MARY. What are you doing?

CHARLEY. Nothing, I'm –

MARY. No, no, you're doing something, your bag's packed and
    now you're –

CHARLEY. –

MARY. You gonna respond?

CHARLEY. Yeah. Okay. Gimme a sec.

MARY. For what?

CHARLEY. To explain.

MARY. To explain why's your bag packed?

CHARLEY. It's not, it's –

MARY. –

CHARLEY. Cos I've been thinking, M.

MARY. And you thought so much your bag got packed?

CHARLEY. –

MARY. What were you thinking about?

CHARLEY. About us.

MARY. Oh yeah?

CHARLEY. And what we're doing.

MARY. And what are we doing?

CHARLEY. Do you wanna sit?

MARY. Not really.

CHARLEY. Or a hug – do you wanna hug?

MARY. Again: no.

CHARLEY. You look like you need one.

MARY. Do I?

CHARLEY. I feel like I need one.

MARY. I can believe that.

CHARLEY. Let's sit, M.

MARY. No, not for me, I'm fine standing – if you wanna sit, sit, but I'm good right here.

　–

And you don't need to stand closer either.

CHARLEY. I wasn't –

MARY. In case you were thinking –

CHARLEY. I'm fine here.

MARY. Cos I don't need a hug.

CHARLEY. Right.

　–

MARY. So what are we doing?

CHARLEY. What?

MARY. You were thinking, Charley, about what we're doing, that's what you said, so now I'm asking you what we're doing.

CHARLEY. We're going in circles.

MARY. And what's that?

CHARLEY. What's a circle?

MARY. Don't take the piss.

CHARLEY. Right, sorry.

I'm sorry.

MARY. Don't apologise; be clear.

CHARLEY. We need a break.

MARY. That's what you mean.

CHARLEY. But you already figured that / cos –

MARY. Cos I saw your bag, yeah.

CHARLEY. I'm sorry.

MARY. For what?

CHARLEY. –

MARY. It's not your fault.

CHARLEY. Didn't say it was my fault.

MARY. You apologised for it.

CHARLEY. I didn't mean –

MARY. Fine. How long you away for then?

CHARLEY. M?

MARY. What?

CHARLEY. Do you think I need to apologise?

MARY. No, I said it's not your fault – how long are you gonna be away?

CHARLEY. Cos I don't think I do need to apologise.

MARY. Good. Neither do I.

CHARLEY. But I think you do, I think that's exactly what you think.

MARY. Fuck's sake Charley.

You talk about circles, these are circles, round and round.

CHARLEY. M.

MARY. How long are you gonna be away?

CHARLEY. I dunno.

MARY. –

CHARLEY. Don't give me that look.

MARY. And don't come near me.

CHARLEY. I'm not.

MARY. You're stepping closer.

CHARLEY. I'm tryna –

MARY. Told you I don't need a hug.

CHARLEY. I wasn't –

MARY. Indefinite, then.

CHARLEY. Excuse me?

MARY. You will be away indefinitely. Is that correct?

CHARLEY. Yes.

MARY. Could be a long time.

CHARLEY. Could be. But I don't want it to be.

MARY. Well that's in your hands.

CHARLEY. What does that mean?

MARY. You're the one leaving – so you decide when you come back.

CHARLEY. That's not how it works.

MARY. How else?

CHARLEY. You don't think it's a two-way street?

That we're in this together, that we decide stuff together.

MARY. I would – but I'm not the one leaving.

CHARLEY. But you're talking about it like I want to do it, like it's my choice.

MARY. Stay here and fix stuff *vs.* leave and let it break – sounds like a choice to me.

CHARLEY. You're being thick now.

MARY. Excuse me?

CHARLEY. And you're –

MARY. What? Talking shite? Talking bollocks?

I'm doing nothing like it, I'm talking sense, Charley, you are the one vanishing, so don't make this about me. These are your problems, go sort them out, come back cleansed.

Take as long as you need.

CHARLEY. As long as I need?

MARY. Now I'm gonna sit.

CHARLEY. *As long as I need.*

MARY. That's what I said, yeah, and I mean it.

CHARLEY. This isn't for me, you know.

MARY. What?

CHARLEY. It's not my time-out – I am giving *you* the time-out. Is that not clear?

MARY. No.

CHARLEY. So let me make it clear.

MARY. Don't use that voice.

CHARLEY. My calm voice?

MARY. It's your pissed-off-patronising voice.

CHARLEY. It is my calm voice, cos I am calm.

I am settled, and in an hour, in a day, in a year, I'll still be using this voice cos I will still be settled.
But I don't think you will be.

MARY. –

CHARLEY. You need rest, M, is all. Need to clear out that brain.

Does that make sense?

MARY. –

CHARLEY. Look at you.

MARY. What?

CHARLEY. Those eyes are opaque.

—
—
—
—
—
—
—
—
—
—
—
—
—
—
—
—
—
—
—
—
—
—
—
—
—
—
—
—
—
—
—
—
—
—
—
—
—
—
—
—
—
—
—
—

ELEVEN

–

–

–

–

CHARLEY. Nice tea.

MARY. Hm?

CHARLEY. It's nice, I said, it's –

MARY. I'll be honest: I didn't think I'd see you...

CHARLEY. This soon?

MARY. Ever.

CHARLEY. Don't be melodramatic.

MARY. I'm not, and don't laugh, I didn't think I would.

And now you're back, and it's kinda nice, and and I'm not
having you leaving.

CHARLEY. Okay.

I mean, I can't really stay long.

MARY. What – eight years gone and you barely manage eight
minutes?

CHARLEY. Frank's in the car so –

MARY. Fuck Frank.

CHARLEY. Mary.

MARY. What?

CHARLEY. I am here with an open mind, alright? Don't take
advantage.

MARY. Your calm voice again.

CHARLEY. Took eight years to get it back, and I am not losing it.

MARY. Fine: let's keep things civilised.

CHARLEY. Let's do just that.

MARY. Do you still love me?

CHARLEY. That's not civilsed.

MARY. Yeah, but secretly, I bet you do.

CHARLEY. And you'd lose that bet.

MARY. Wouldn't be so sure.

CHARLEY. I don't still love you, Mary – otherwise I'd've called, wouldn't I?

MARY. Guess you would've, yeah.

–

CHARLEY. Look, I should probably –

MARY. C'mon.

CHARLEY. No, Frank's with the baby and –

MARY. Can I meet him?

CHARLEY. I'd rather not, I don't want…

MARY. What?

CHARLEY. This isn't –

We are not reuniting, Mary – I dunno what you thought when we spoke, but it's not that.

MARY. I thought you just wanted to say *hi*.

CHARLEY. Well, yeah, it is that, but –

MARY. But.

CHARLEY. Two things I wanted to tell you – that's it.

Frank said you deserved to know, and now you know, and that's enough for me.

I'm sorry if you thought it was more, if you thought –

I dunno.

It's just two things I wanted to tell you

MARY. You got married again, you got a child.

CHARLEY. and that's all.

MARY. That's all?

CHARLEY. Yeah.

MARY. Nothing else?

CHARLEY. No, and you know now / so –

MARY. So you can leave?

CHARLEY. Exactly.

MARY. And that's it?

CHARLEY. It was nice to see you.

MARY. No.

CHARLEY. Excuse me?

MARY. You don't get to –

CHARLEY. Walk out?

MARY. Shouldn't be able to.

CHARLEY. Why not?

MARY. Fuck's sake, Charley, you can't just –

CHARLEY. Here it is.

MARY. Here's what?

CHARLEY. Why I left.

MARY. Oh piss off.

CHARLEY. In a nutshell.

MARY. Don't make this about me.

CHARLEY. Who else is it about?

MARY. It's about us.

CHARLEY. No, it's always about you,

MARY. Fifty-fifty.

CHARLEY. like it ever was.

MARY. It always was.

CHARLEY. About us?

MARY. ALWAYS.

CHARLEY. Fuck me.

MARY. NOT ANY MORE.

CHARLEY. Very good, very good, very childish, very –

MARY. Funny.

CHARLEY. I'm off, I'm leaving.

MARY. Why? I was enjoying that argument.

–

What's he called?

CHARLEY. Who, Frank? Frank's called Frank.

MARY. Your kid – what's he called?

CHARLEY. It's a she.

She's a she.

MARY. Fine: she. Your daughter. What's your daughter called?

CHARLEY. Not now, Mary.

MARY. What, Chaz?

CHARLEY. Look, we've had a catch-up, we've had a nice chat
/ and –

MARY. We've had a *quick* chat.

CHARLEY. And now we're winding each other up.

MARY. You don't think that.

CHARLEY. No, you're right: I think *you're* winding *me* up.

MARY. It's a simple question.

CHARLEY. Let's leave it.

MARY. I just wanna know.

CHARLEY. Why? You're suddenly curious?

MARY. No, cos I care, is all.

CHARLEY. Right. And what else is new with you?

MARY. Oh I don't know, not much I guess, but I'm not the one who stopped being gay and married a man called Frank.

CHARLEY. Okay.

Fine.

I see.

MARY. What?

What are you seeing with X-Ray vision?

CHARLEY. I'm off.

MARY. You've said that before.

CHARLEY. Yeah, well, this time –

MARY. Tell me her name before you go.

–

Go on: easy question, easy answer.

CHARLEY. It's not, it's more than that.

MARY. It's simple.

CHARLEY. It is complex.

MARY. Why? Is it difficult to pronounce?

CHARLEY. Funny.

MARY. I'm just curious.

CHARLEY. Petulant.

MARY. Fine, I am petulant.

CHARLEY. And you claw at me, Mary.

MARY. And I will keep clawing till I know.

CHARLEY. Ask me then.

MARY. What's she called?

CHARLEY. Miriam.

MARY. Charley'll never know why but the room goes dead.
   She's not wanted. She mumbles *bye*, she pats my shoulder, she smiles, and then she's gone and I'm alone in the stagnant air.

I want company, but even the telly's broken.

She's got company: a Miriam.

Which stirs up shit I don't wanna go through, blows up shit
I thought I'd forgotten.

About who deserves what and why and I push down, push it
down, push it down hard.

Hold it there.

Mary is perfectly still.

Then Mary starts to shake, her hand wobbles, and she tries to
hold it steady.

Mary breathes out, pushes all the air out her lungs and sags,
empty.

Mary is perfectly still – until she goes blue.

–

Mary's throat opens, vacuums in the air around her.

Fuck.

My head's –

Is it hot?

It's hot, it is really hot.

Mary goes to the window, tries to open it.

Won't open.

And I want to smash it.

Fucker's been stuck for years.

And my brain's –

Come on.

Mary forces it.

Mary pushes harder, the window doesn't give.

Mary smacks the glass.

Come ON.

Mary smacks the glass and her hands smash through.

Air blasts into the room

and for a moment it's the most refreshing things I've ever –
breathe it –

until I see blood pouring out from my –

wrists, hands, glaring, red, shards.

I grab a T-shirt, try to block up the troughs of –

Mary gags.

And my brain –

Doesn't work –

Need something more –

Mary rushes through to the kitchen.

Frozen peas.
Mary throws open the freezer door, scrambles inside, searching
for –
But I'm knocking everything out, head's not on proper, I'm
knocking things out, onto the floor, chips, lasagne,
bag for life, bag for life.
Is that?
One of the bags is open.
Is that – fingers.
Haven't seen them in –
Haven't *thought* about them in –
Mary looks down at them.
Foot
Hand
Green wire.
Her own arm
Gorged
And my head's washed out,
phone,
ring,
door rushed open
is that –
need to –
phone
Charley?
ambulance,
rush,
siren,
A&E
drowsed,
lag
sit, nurse, sit
sleep
ragged
–
–
–
–

TWELVE

Up
Mary.
Doctor.
12 p.m. – I think
Clock's blurry.
Doctor's surgery, quiet office.
I'm bandaged.
Mary examines her arms and my brain woozes.
The doctor, he's saying,
something,
I think he says
something like:

–

Ms Malek.
You'll be feeling numb at the moment, that's the painkillers.
The cuts you've received to your forearms and wrists are deep.
The nerve have been cut. Completely. And that requires a long
recovery process. Even if the nerves manage to repair
themselves, and the odds are slim, it's painful. And I can't be
sure if you'll ever fully recover the feeling in your right hand.
I'm sorry.
Uh
Before we go on, I need to know if cuts were administered by
accident or whether...

–

Okay.
I understand.
Because if they were not by accident, Ms Malek, I would have
to –

–

No. Okay.
I understand.
When your wife brought you in –

–

Ex-wife. Apologies.

–

Your ex-wife brought you in and she said you were flustered,
you two had some kind of confrontation, and it's only natural in
that situation to have feelings that may take over...

If your response is certain then I don't have to bring it up again.
–

Thank you.

–

We have options, for you, Ms Malek.
Artificial replacements.

–

Then the doctor leans back on his chair, reaches over to a
drawer under his desk, and pulls out a clear plastic bag.
He holds it up.
Mary watches the bag.
He's still talking but I only half-listen
Experimental phase
Perfectly safe
Years of testing
Short recovery time
cos inside the bag is a green plastic wire.
And there's a flash piercing my eye – a glint of gold, and
I recognise an image buried in my brain.
A tiny diamond logo, catching the sun.
What's he calling it?
An artificial nerve.
I'm trying to piece him together.
You tested it?
But he doesn't give me an answer.
He smiles – the same smiliest smile that he did to me eight
years ago in the same office when he told me my Miriam
was dead.
On who, who did you test it on?
He's still silent, still smiling.
I stare at him – he's looking through me.
Then he drops the wire back on the desk, and becomes very
serious, he places a form in front of me – CONFIDENTIAL –
and slides it over.
Mary signs it without looking.
Even he's not too happy with how quickly I sign it, but I sign it.
I want in.

–

He tells me he's going to administer the anaesthetic.
In here?
In here.

It's easier: people get nervous, frightened, so better to knock
them out before they can even think about it.

He's right: I'm starting to get nervous.

I'm trying not to think, I'm watching that green wire, the fine
strings of copper.

So when he tells me to stick out my wrist I find it's settled in his
palm without me noticing.

Tight grip.

Anaesthetic.

Prick into my arm – lightning quick.

We need to be swift, he declares, anaesthetic'll hit soon and
before I know it, I'll be operated on, awake, recovered.

–

We wait.

I feel fine.

He's smiling.

It's too much.

He asks if I'm feeling alright.

Fine.

I'm fine.

But I should be woozy.

Mary sits up straight.

Doctor's mind is whirring.

Painkillers. Painkillers fuck with it sometimes, you need a
stronger dose – and with that he's off, out the room.

Door slams, Mary's up.

His desk, find his papers.

She flits through them all, checking names, numbers anything.

Feeling a bit woozy, start of the anaesthetic.

Push on, Mary pushes on.

Keep searching. Numbers, becoming blurs – black letters, black
numbers, fading into grey smudges.

Mary shakes her head.

Clearer, crisper.

Then back to grey.

Keep searching.

Footsteps down the corridor.

Is someone coming? Is someone –

SHIT.

–

Keep searching.

Still grey.
I'm woozier, I'm –
Keep searching.
And then: Mary stops.
A bit of text that sticks out, I see solid black letters, solid black
numbers on the starkest white background.
201-MMCD
M-M-C-D
Is that –
Mary Malek Charley Dimmock
Could be.
Must be.
Can't not be.
It's –
Miriam.
Door swings open, foot steps in, anaesthetic kicks in.
Ms Malek?
Out like a light.
–
–
–
–

THIRTEEN

On my tongue, there's sand.
Dusk
Tide's in, it's a clump of wet sand.
And my feet –
They are freezing, there's water swashed over them.
It's raining, only fine rain, and my hand is lying, detached,
flopped out in front of me.
And then it jumps up and scuttles over me, no warning.
It smells sweaty – but that could be the sewage – and clings
onto my face, and I have to rip it off.
Mary clutches onto the hand.
Fingers all wriggling about.
She holds it up to the light.

Mary looks at her wrist: a stump.
Then Mary looks back to her hand.
She draws the two together – like a spacecraft docking.
The parts click into place.
There's a buzz of electricity.
Mary is frazzled with the energy, with the pain.
Then she stands.
Mary sways.
Mary holds steady.
She takes a step forward.
Pauses.
Then another.
Electricity buzzing through her.
Pushing her up and –
Mary's floating.
Up in the air.
Across beaches, across grassy fields, down the A259, above
SUVs and autocars, past the roundabout, third left, straight on,
hard right.
Someone shouts Mary's name.
It's soft, from offstage.
Mary's still floating – down a country lane, swerving to avoid
the cars.
And again.
Turn off and follow signs to the hospital.
And again.
Fog descends.
She follows its light –
The shout, again – firmer this time.
But the hospital, a halo, burning –
Mary.
Louder.
She looks down at her hand, it's translucent.
Wind rushing past her head.
Above the hospital now, and dropping down.
Mary's going to smash into the roof, crumble onto concrete,
closer –
But she passes through, a ghost, and her body drifts, through the
fifth floor, fourth floor, third, second, first,
and keeps dropping down through –
Ms Malek.

Into the ground –
Ms Malek
Into the –
MARY.
Flashing my eyes open.

–

–

–

–

FOURTEEN

I'm in the waiting room.
And I'm – I'm hungry – it's dinner time
I think –
It's – I'm in this quiet corner and this nurse, she's in front of
me, she's mowing through words:
Operation a success.
I need rest – movement must be kept to a minimum.
The new nerve is sensitive, it can overload – which means the
nerve could burst into flames, inside my body.
And they didn't tell me that before.
Or maybe they did but I didn't read the form properly.
Tryna take it in.
The nurse is in front of me jabberin' and I wonder maybe if
I blink hard enough and stare hard enough she'll shut up and let
me be.
She doesn't.
And all through my head is MMCD
I want to speak to the doctor.
That's what I decide I want.
And I let the sentence out – the nurse looks back, puzzled.
Mary's fuzzy.
Mary double-blinks.
I think the nurse is telling me to go home – but the doctor
walks by.
Mary's eyes refocus, past the nurse, onto the doctor: he's
walking in slow motion across the room, eyes all flash, teeth all
bared, arm stretched out to greet a patient.

I'm gonna interrupt him, I wanna speak to him.

Then Mary's eyes flick across the room – and I settle on that patient, and it's Charley.

Shit.

Charley.

Standing, awkwardly – and she's never an athlete, but she looks weak: she needs to support herself as she gets up, I wonder if she's ill and I want to run over and comfort her, ask if she's okay then –

Mary's face drops.

And it hits.

Charley's got one hand stretched out, balancing herself, and another on her belly.

–

Another one.

Can't keep her legs shut.

Charley's shaking hands with the doctor – she's being deliberate, she's patting her tummy and laughing and flicking her hair like she's got a siren attached to her head that blares

BABY

Good. Good for her.

Mary stands.

Charley can't see me like this.

Corner the doctor later; hide from Charley now.

Mary takes a step back.

And another and she keeps stepping back until she hits the wall.

Her right elbow hits first – thwacks against plasterboard, and it's agony.

Mary clutches onto her arm, holds it still.

The arms's numb for a moment.

But then the nails start digging in, the pain's getting worse.

Another yelp.

Both at once – the doctor and Charley – they look over.

Eye contact with the doctor.

I can't read his face – is he calm? Or terrified? Or anything?

Keep staring.

I try to ignore Charley and I focus on the doctor.

His face is guilty and he can't hide it. He's talking to Charley, trying to look professional, trying not to get distracted.

–

Then my brain twitches – fuck Charley: confront the doctor.

So I bounce off the wall, a line, straight, cross the room, over to him.

I'm gonna confront him, I am gonna make a scene.

Charley's seen me, she's calling out – *M* – but I ignore her.

Mary's pace quickens.

I've got demands and swearing and threats all hurled at the doctor who is schtum and I am blaring out

M – M – C – D

again, drilling it in, cos I am demanding to know where my daughter is.

Pain builds in my arm as Charley gets involved and her words now are jagged and rattling, and the doctor is left to scramble beneath us as we ROAR.

The nurse intervenes.

She has to pull me back, and Charley throws her hands in the air, and the doctor apologises to her and snarls at me and is gone.

Whoosh.

Before he arrived.

And I watch him.

I make a note of which door he passes through.

Mary is restrained by the nurse, guided to a seat.

Mary breathes, the nurse puts a hand on Mary's shoulder, checks that she's alright, but is told to fuck off.

So Mary sits, patient.

Charley sits near Mary, but not with her.

Pause, for a long time.

She gonna speak first?

I've got no words, not for her.

And Charley's got no words for me.

Charley rubs her belly, Charley sighs, like she can't be bothered.

Then she's off – out – not a word.

Mary eye's follow Charley's figure, but only for a moment.

And then I peer around the room, check the nurse is gone, check that I am anonymous.

Mary heaves herself up.

She focuses on the door, the one the doctor passed through.

Her arm throbs, she clutches it.

Mary takes a step towards the door.

Careful steps, one by one, each step a little –

Ow.
Pain.
step
ow
pain
step
ow
Arm steady, keep it level.
step
ow
pain
Christ alive.
Hand to the door, peek over the shoulder, pass through: and
there he is.
He's ducking into a storage unit.
And I follow
–
–
–
–

FIFTEEN

The doctor refuses to speak.
10 p.m.
Not an honest word; just excuses.
Madness. He says.
Idiocy. He balks.
He lies.
So I got furious – I am furious.
And now I'm breathing on his face, my eyes, pricked enough to
pierce his skin, and I'm gonna stay right up close.
I clutch his neck and am close enough to lick his bulging
eyeballs.
He is trembling.
What is MMCD?
Tell me it's my Miriam.
No response.

The storage unit is a giant freezer, tucked into the basement of the building. It's walk-in, deluxe, cleaner than any ward I've seen, draining enough energy for a town.

There are shelves of dull metal, packed with ice, stacked with containers, crammed with organs and limbs and bones, preserved solid until they're needed.

I followed him inside, jammed the door shut, and I asked him, politely, to tell me what MMCD means.

No clue, he said.

Bullshit, I said: Mary Malek Charley Dimmock

And then he looked confused, and he started rambling, aggressive, patronising, told me I'm mad, told me my brain's not plugged in right, told me told me told me and his words kept hitting me till I silenced him by grabbing his throat, pushing him up against the wall, and now that's exactly where we stand.

If I didn't want to kill him, this'd be the closest I ever got to kissing a guy.

The doctor struggles, tries to shift his body out from Mary's grip.

Mary clutches tighter.

We look at each other.

We breathe steadily, heavily.

And I decide I will speak again, calm, I will ask –

A beep.

Shrill, sudden.

Automatic, the doctor reaches for his pocket, but Mary pushes him harder up against the wall – I tell him he's not moving.

He begs me, it's urgent, an emergency: he's being paged – but no one's had a pager for decades, and his eyes are flashing at me, lying to me, shameless.

Grip tightens.

I tell him this is the part where he gives me answers.

I tell him I found papers on his desk: 201-MMCD.

I tell him I know what that means.

I tell him about the foot.

I tell him about the hand.

I tell him about the green wire.

And then I ask him, blunt, pointed: who are you experimenting on?

Sweat.

The doctor starts to sweat.

It's below zero and the man is *sweating*. He looks panicked.
Naughty-schoolkid-cheating-husband panic.

And now he's really struggling, trying to reach down to
his pocket, trying to hide something, and he's almost
overpowering me.

Almost –

But Mary twists her grip and the doctor flinches in agony.
His arm smacks into a container, a box crashing to the floor:
limbs, shards of blood, bone.

A leg bone

ripped out of flesh

and Mary picks it up.

The doctor's heading to the door, Mary thuds the bone onto his
back.

He collapses. He lets out a strange wail.

I tell him once more I want answers and he looks at me.

It's like his whole face is wobbling, incoherent, jelly.

I wait for him to speak.

But the doctor stays bent double, lifting up his head, his eyes
looking for mercy, but the leg bone, I have decided, is a dagger,
now, aimed at his eyes.

Easing closer.

His eyes wet.

Mary shakes.

His eyes wet.

Mary pummels the thick bone into his left socket.

Doctor's mouth is wide open, his teeth are ragged, his tongue
vibrates and he should be screaming but he's on mute – silent,
as I watch his face drift to the floor, his body crumpling under
him.

A cold thump, then quiet.

Mary stands tall. Blood pumping.

Never felt this – blood, warm, rippling, physically pumping
through me, like I'm overflowing with gloopy red energy. And
the doctor's whimpering's drained to nothing, so there's just my
hoarse breath, and the hum of the fridge, and my hand's shaking.

–

There it is again: a

BEEP.

From where?

BEEP.
A phone?
BEEP.
Older than that, analogue.
BEEP.
And then I see the flash from the doctor's belt.
BEEP.
It is a pager.
BEEP.
Mary notices a message flashing on the pager screen.
WARD 201
That's all it says, and suddenly I'm freezing.
201
201-MMCD
The doctor refused to provide answers, but his pager does.
And I chase.
–
–
–
–

SIXTEEN

The door to the ward: an embossed, matted, clean *2 – 0 – 1*
Midnight
Mary swings the door open.
Mary falters.
I take it in in gulps.
Gulp 1:
Rows of beds, humans splayed out on them, a flood of beeping
and medical equipment all smashing into me at once.
Gulp 2:
The humans are sliced open, their insides are exposed, but
instead of muscles there are wires, tiny gyroscopes, pumps and
tubes, all connected up to monitors.
Gulp 3:
Whole bodies cut down the centre everything inside replaced
with plastic and metal.

Gulp 4:

They're all female. They are all pre-pubescent.

Gulp 5:

The smell is urine and detergent.

Gulp 6:

A sound of pain cuts beneath it all, deep, far too deep for an
eight-year-old, or six-year-old, or whatever she is.

I zone in on her.

Far side, halfway down.

Mary approaches.

Noise is pouring out her mouth.

And I'm helpless. The fuck can I do?

Still, she's watching me.

Or – I think she is – it's a camera lens not an eye, but it's aimed
at me, and a beep runs, from her eye down to this mechanical
voice box, and a flashing light goes from red to green as a
gravel screech comes out her mouth.

It's a scream.

It's not human, but it's a scream and it's panicked, so I need to
act, I need to –

Mary remains still.

Mary's eyes flicker.

Then, above her bed, she notices something: a small, white
piece of card, on which, in a slim font, is a code:

201-DMIM

I spin round – another bed, another code:

201-MDID

And the next bed

201-LDXI

And the next

201-MIVI

And the next

201-DICD

And I'm starting to get lost, codes and numbers are all shifting
into one, need to keep track of them, have to concentrate but
still the sound of screaming

201-DMIM, louder this time, louder than we've heard it.

Electric scream of –

ZZZZZZZZZZAAAARGH!

No.

Keep MMCD in my head.

Mary
Malek
Charley
Dimmock
Don't lose her.
Mary's eyes scan each bed.
Scan each little placard.
But it's a jumble of –
CIMVLXDMVLMCXIVLIDMMCDXI –
Was that?
Is that?
MMCD
Eyes shift down.
Bed's empty.
–

Imprint of a child, an abandoned monitor, loose wires.
It's empty.
I watch the bed, close my eyes, squeeze them tight, then open
them and it's still empty and I shudder, and I repeat the cycle.
My arm's in pain, it feels hot.
Blinking, opening.
Blinking, opening.
Empty bed.
And I will –
And I will –
And the door flies open.
It's the doctor.
He's got an eye patch.
And he looks like a wild medicinal pirate as he stumbles
towards me.
Mary steps back.
He approaches.
Mary steps back.
Ms Malek.
MS MALEK.
He tells me I can't be in here but that's pretty fucking obvious.
He tells me he's furious.
He's got his hands raised, he's trying to calm me, but he's just
making me alert and scared.
My eyes are fixed on him and I'm terrified of him and I just
need a threat, something to make him back off, so I shift

myself, closer to the nearest bed, and my left hand reaches
down and I grab onto a bundle of wires.

Raw in my hand.

Mary looks at what she's grabbed.

It is the throat of 201-DMIM.

And the doctor's right in front of me now – he's lunged twenty
feet closer so he's almost breathing on me.

And 201-DMIM, she's screaming in pain, and I feel sorry for
her, almost, but she's more robot than human

and maybe if I do rip out these wires it'll shut her up or –

Don't know.

Can't think.

Grip tightens.

Can't think.

I'm locked into staring with the doctor.

He looks scared.

Like he just wants to do his job.

Like he's a kind man.

Or a weak man.

I'm a human, he's a mouse and I know who's more scared of
who.

So I make my demands.

Where is she?

Last chance.

Where is she?

His eye blinks.

–

There's a pause for a microsecond.

He hesitates and I'm furious and I don't speak again I just –

Mary rips at the wires.

There's a burst of electricity.

Mary explodes back with shock.

Mary –

–

–

–

–

SEVENTEEN

Bzzzzzzzzzzzzzzzzzzzzzzzzzzzzzzzzzzzzzzzzzzzzzzzzzzzzzzzzzzzzzzap.
BzzzzzzzzzzzzzzzzzzzzzzzzzzzzzzzzzzzzzAP.
BZAP
BZAP
Bzzzzzzzzzzzzzzzzzzzzzzzzzzz –
THWACK.
Mary's arm swings at nothing.
bzzzzzzzzzzzzzzz –
Swats again, her eyes prick –
Bzzzzzzzzzz –
The doctor coughs. Then there's silence and all I can focus on is
six thin legs tickling my check, and I slap at them and jerk up
and –
No windows so I can't tell how long I've been here.
I'm groggy.
My head is –
Spinning.
Mary's arm aches.
Spinning so I have to look around twice to make sure I'm in the
same place.
Same ward, same stench – that urine-detergent smell.
But everything's different.
All the wires are gone.
The same patients, the same girls – but they've been stitched
back up, there are beeps and whirs, but it's not the droning
threat of electric power.
Mary stands up.
Mary walks around.
She approaches one of the beds, sees a young girl – she's
translucent, apart from tiny red splotches, dotted down her arm,
across her neck, up her thigh.
Mary looks up, tries to check the patient's code – but the little
white card is gone.
They're all gone.
Mary goes to speak.
The doctor cuts her off.
He wants to play a game – he tells me.
And he's suddenly movie-villain sinister.
He wants me to find my Miriam.
He doesn't use the word Miriam.

He uses child, kid, *it*.

It's a dare.

He is daring me.

The doctor speaks with calm and precision.

–

201-MMCD is a patient, 201 is a ward number, MMCD an identity code.

The patient was removed from this ward, but has now been returned.

The patient has undergone experimental treatment, fitted, from a young age, with artificial nerves, with a replacement heart, and more.

The patient's life has been preserved.

You believe the patient is your daughter.

So find her.

–

And it's the simplest game in the world.

Find my daughter.

I know what I'm looking for and I search for her: I will be systematic, I will be consistent, I will search thoroughly for Miriam.

Examine each child, till I find the one whose face belongs to me, whose nose and eyes and mouth are a mirror to mine.

My heart's pulsing harder.

My eyes are flitting across details.

The shape of a face, of your own DNA.

Unmistakeable.

The doctor watches on.

Mary's heart beats harder.

Adrenalin.

Only so many beds left to search, must be –

Not here; try there.

Not here; try there.

Mary's eyes rotating through the bodies – small girls contorted, healing on their beds.

She's trying to notice details but coming up short.

Onto the next bed.

And try again.

Search.

The next.

The next.

Then she hits the final bed.

Last chance.

Miriam.

Pause.

She's trying to recognise a nose, or an eye colour, or a neckline
or –

But there's nothing.

Maybe she's fading.

And if I can barely recognise my own –

Mary goes stiff.

She keeps staring at the child in front of her.

I will find something.

Buck teeth, or a wonky eye, or a nose that's –

The doctor's right behind me.

Well?

He's smug.

He wants me to promise that this will put a rest to everything.

Then he mutters something about legal action.

He's threatening me and he's not even batting an eye –

His eye patch is gone.

Just in that second it strikes me.

And I don't know –

But it's healed –

And he's –

Is he –

Ms Malek

His voice sucking me in.

–

Ms Malek, you and your ex-wife, the child you had together
was a boy.

Were you aware?

–

And he takes out some pink papers that are supposed to be
proof of something.

And his smile is meek.

Mary slopes downwards.

The doctor squeezes her shoulder.

I feel –

Nausea.

I want a seat.

I want fresh air.

I want –

The doctor pushes Mary towards the exit.

And I give in.

I let him lead me – numb and passive.

I start to notice pains in my body.

I'm gripping my arm and he asks me if it hurts but I shrug.

We're floating away and –

Mary hears something.

Soft, beneath the low whir of machines.

Mary shakes the feeling away.

Then again.

Can't quite make it out.

And again.

Mama.

She thinks she hears

Mama.

Again.

She looks to the doctor.

He hasn't noticed – good, keep it like that, stay calm.

Mama.

Stay calm.

Is that –

But Mary can't.

Miriam.

He asks me if I'm alright and I nod *fine fine fine fine fine fine* –

Mama.

She fixes on it.

Then another shout.

MAMA.

I want to look back, but I can't cos then the doctor'll know
something's going on, so I keep my head stiff, locked straight
ahead, and when we get to the door I –

Mary lets the doctor exit first and once he's through –

Kick and a slam.

Lock him out.

Mary grabs a chair, slots it against the door, wedges it under the
handle.

Then turns back to the room.

Beds lined up in front of her.

I can hear the doctor beating on the door, trying to get in.

But I can also hear: MAMA.

There.

Located.

Across the room.

And this time there's no error – Mary runs straight to her daughter.

201-MMCD

She's writhing, screaming out, desperate.

She's got her mother's glorious buck teeth – shining bright.

And Miriam sees her mother.

But it's not the look Mary wants, it's confused, like she's forgotten we are one.

I smile and I kiss her and I –

Mary hugs her.

Really tight: Play-Doh.

She's squirming under me, so I hug her tighter.

Miriam pulls back, I grip her shoulders.

Mary locks her eyes into Miriam's.

Are you hearing me?

Can you hear anything?

Can you hear ME?

It's a nod, I get a nod.

Good.

Good.

The door on the far wall is being rattled.

Can you walk?

Miriam can't respond – her mouth is locked shut.

Mary touches her daughter's face.

–

The door is rattling harder.

Mary grabs Miriam's shoulders, makes her sit up.

Mary snaps back the white sheets, swipes Miriam's legs out from the bed.

Mary hugs her daughter again.

Then Mary whispers in Miriam's ear:

You trust me, don't you?

–

And my eyes are searching Miriam's face – she barely reacts.

But the teeth.

Those goofy buck teeth.

Are mine.

I look around for a wheelchair, there isn't one.

Shit.

The door's rattling harder.

Mary kneels in front of her daughter.

Mary takes her daughter's hand, squeezes.

I tell her she's gonna have to walk.

CAN YOU DO THAT?

MIRIAM?

CAN YOU DO THAT FOR MUMMY?

Doesn't comprehend it.

So I grab her hands and pull her up.

Miriam flinches.

I think it hurts her.

She falls back, shields herself, curls up.

But she has to move.

Mary grabs Miriam's hands, harder this time, and pulls her daughter up.

Miriam's on both feet.

Mary holds out her right arm and Miriam puts all her weight onto it.

They stand steady for a moment.

Mary's arm feels hot, feels like it's overheating, but she bites through the pain of it.

Mary takes a step forward – Miriam follows.

And another.

Mary's arm is boiling up.

But they're making progress.

They're stepping forward.

One by one.

But Miriam's legs start to give a little.

She clutches hard at Mary's right arm.

Then Miriam slips, clings on harder.

Miriam crumbles onto that right arm and Mary feels it, the pain's too much, she lets out –

ARRRRRRGH.

Mary feels sparks pulsating through her.

The heat's unbearable.

It's boiling her from inside.

There's red, blue, white heat pouring out her skin, singeing and burning her.

Mary buckles.

The sound of her clattering to the floor.

And as Mary falls:

The door bursts open.
And as Mary falls:
Miriam falls with her.
And as Mary falls:
Her arm catches in bright flames, bursting her body open, she's
filled with pain and steel and there's a chorus around her:
MADAM
MADAM
STAY BACK
STAY BACK
chaos
hundreds of nurses thousands of doctors all streaming in
surrounding Mary and Miriam
all with hands and arms and limbs all everywhere all at once
manic
trying to be calm
but they're manic
they're manic
MADAM
MADAM
arm's burst off
watching insides being torn out
replaced
in the pain
delusional
hot
sweating
hot
pain
the world's been rubbed out
only whirls of screams and
heat
MADAM
MADAM
and Miriam's convulsing
her body's chucked around
nurse to doctor to doctor to nurse
trying to save her
hand
busy
hand

work
WORK
fucking
WORK
and SAVE her
her body's
not
not –
i'm sorry
don't say sorry
i'm sorry
she's not –
not
not WHAT?
NOT WHAT?
not responding
too active
body's too
over –
overworked
overheated
and
MADAM
MADAM
BACK
miriam explodes
–
in slow motion
–
she explodes
GET BACK
she explodes
in mary's retina
she sees limbs torn from limbs with live wires burning out and
up and
globules of limbs of fat of muscles of wires
and miriam
gone
and
miriam
is –

–
–
–
–

EIGHTEEN

The weather.
Dark clouds, could be midday, midnight, Mary's in a trance, the
TV drones.
The weather. Brewing up again. Biggest storm in years.
Electrical storms.
Rain storms.
Fuck off storms.
Storm Miriam is hitting. That time of year and Storm Miriam is
hitting.
The Met Office has today announced.
Has officially named –
The storm.
On its way.
Up the Channel.
Prevailing winds.
Important.
Complex.
Meteorological terms.
Clear the beaches, clear the seas, prepare for the deluge.
The sound of rain can be heard. It's the start of something.
Not soft, but we can tell it's going to build.
And it does.
It builds up.
The rain lashes, covers the stage, soaks it.
Winds blow through.
Vacuum cleaner.
Bursts through and it's deafening.
Sucking us all in.
Into the swell.
Louder.
No, LOUDER.

SO YOU HAVE TO SHOUT ABOVE IT.
TO BE HEARD.
GAILS.
BLUSTERING THROUGH US.
RAINS HITTING HARDER.
SOLID SLEET.
ICE SMASHING INTO US.
TEARING OUT FACES.
AND AS SUDDEN AS IT STARTED WE'RE MET WITH –
–
–
–
–

NINETEEN

Calm.

Dawn.

Mary lies in her bed.

She's at home, and there's a half-light tiptoeing through the window.

It's definitely a sunrise or a sunset but we can't figure out which.

Outside, the storm is over.

There's a card resting on her bedside table – it's from Charley.

The scene is idyllic.

Mary snores, stirs, wakes.

She sits up in bed.

She notices the card but ignores it.

She looks at her right arm.

It's normal.

Apart from –

Little stitches, minuscule bruises battered onto the surface of her skin.

Mary traces the stitches around her arm, up to her hand, down to her elbow.

She's terrified of moving the arm too much, terrified of the pain returning.

But it feels fine, numb even.

So, she flexes it, stretches out those fingers, lets them move around, and they're agile.

Relief.

Mary's up.

She goes to the window, watches the sky for a moment – she decides it's morning.

The sky is completely cleared.

It's purple, getting lighter – like a bruise fading – into a shining blue.

She opens the window.

The wind's not bitter any more.

It won't bite.

Mary looks down to the beach.

It's covered in debris.

Natural and artificial: splinters of houses trees cars, all sprinkled with seaweed and dried salt.

Mary savours the stillness.

She leaves the room, heads down to the beach.

–

–

–

–

TWENTY

Completely still in the

Daytime

She's been asleep for days, she thinks, or maybe weeks.

And Mary still feels tired.

Mary trudges on.

The sand beneath looks more like muck and

she has to work her way round rubbish, bits of bark, scrap metal.

Mary reaches the edge of the sea.

Mary watches the sea water – it's filthy.

She wonders if she could dissolve into the sea.

Like all the bits of sewage do, all the waste – no one would notice.

It's been years since anyone swam in this water.
But Mary's attention is caught by something.
Her head flicks to one side.
Staring up at her, like a rodent.
A pair of eyes.
Familiar eyes – she thinks, she's not sure – but then she
recognises those buck teeth.
She smiles.
Miriam's head – wires and guts pouring out of her neck.
Mary watches it for a moment.
Then looks around, makes sure no one else is watching.
Mary pulls a bag out of her pocket – it's plastic and it says Lidl
on it.
She picks up the head and places it inside.
There are wires strewn around and she gathers them up as well,
stuffs them into the bag.
Mary keeps searching.
–
Mary is sewing.
It's late, later.
Sewing calms her completely.
Each stitch is little relief, relaxes her bones.
So Mary sews in front of the TV (still broken).
Mary sews in the garden (when it's sunny).
Mary sews at the kitchen table.
Every now and then she goes to the freezer, defrosts something
for herself, and then it's back to sewing.
Mary sews in bed.
It gives her a chance to make plans.
Mary will probably wind down her teaching work.
Mary could look for another partner.
Mary might move house.
Stitch after stitch, Mary keeps going.
And Mary looks down at her handiwork.
She's proud of it.
–
Mary stands, stretches her body out.
Early morning
She walks around, takes a quick break, maybe she goes down to
the beach again.
Maybe she goes out to pick up supplies.

But whenever she's not sewing, it's all she can do to think
of sewing.
She gets nervous when she's not.
Mary fidgets.
Mary keeps sewing.
It's becoming an obsession.
She's connecting all the pieces together.
It's taking her days, maybe it's taking her weeks.
Mary keeps sewing.
Until, she thinks, *finally*.
Finally, thinks she might be finished sewing.
Mary looks down at her work.
She is dead proud.
Mary lets a huge smile spread across her face.
On the table in front of her, perfectly whole and complete, is
Miriam.
All Miriam's different limbs, body parts, wires, everything.
It has all been sewn back together and Mary smiles down at her
rebuilt daughter.
Mary smiles so much her buck teeth show.
–
Mary sleeps.
Witching hour.
She's in her bedroom.
There's a bang from downstairs, and Mary is woken up,
startled.
She listens out: again: a bang.
She's terrified, for a moment.
But there's only one person it could be.
Charley.
Another bang.
Mary calls out: CHARLEY?!
Silence for a moment, then another bang.
Jesus wept, Mary stands.
Mary scratches at her eyes, which hang half-open.
Another bang – from the kitchen.
Mary follows the sound.
In the kitchen is a figure, half-lit by the moonlight.
Charley?
What are you –
Like she doesn't hear a thing.

Mary hovers.
And the fridge is open so Mary goes to shut it but –
Her toe catches something – it's a wire, stranded on the floor.
Mary looks down: it's not just one wire, it's a mass of them, and
they writhe across the floor, a trail leading to –
Miriam.
With wires dripping out of her skin.
Miriam, alive, naked, breathing, standing right in front of her.
Miriam turns around.
Mary's dumb.
Just for that moment – nothing crosses her mind.
Nothing, until the moonlight snaps her out of it and
Mary holds out her arms, approaches Miriam, and Miriam
doesn't resist, she doesn't flinch – so Mary is able to feel and
clutch onto and hold her daughter like never before.
Mary squeeeeezes Miriam into the tightest hug.
They are Play-Doh together.
And Miriam feels perfect in her arms, fits perfectly in her arms.
Mary starts humming.
Miriam starts to giggle.
Mary hums louder.
Mary cradles Miriam.

Charley-bit-bitter, age-old
weary grump, sat lonesome
in torment and gave me
the hump

So cow-big-bigger, with a
slumping fat teet, wormed
on over and crushed her
small feet

And bird-small-smaller, with
hard sharp beak, pecked
at her skin, all flaking
and weak

While pig-pork-porker, tail curled,
belly fat, nuzzled
a fat nose up and inside
her twat

But Mary-joy-joyer, holding
on tight, clutched hard to
my darling and squealed
with delight

Do you like that, Miriam?
I can hear Miriam's joyful giggle so don't need an answer.
Mary smiles.
And she is so happy.
She is so happy.

–

–

–

–

THE STRONGBOX

Stephanie Jacob

The Strongbox was first performed at VAULT Festival, London, on 28 February 2018, with the following cast:

MA   Joanna Wake
KAT   Stephanie Jacob
MAUDIE   Hannah Morley

Director   Lucy Richardson
Scenography &   Jelmer Tuinstra
  Lighting Design
Sound Design   Lex Kosanke

Characters

MA, *a woman in her seventies, a Londoner*
KAT, *her daughter, in her forties*
MAUDIE, *a girl aged seventeen, from Bristol*

The play is set in London, present day.

ONE

A table set for two: soup, bread, two apples, a sharp knife.
MAUDIE, *wearing a McDonald's cap, stands behind* MA*'s chair.* MA *sits opposite* KAT, *in dressing gown and slippers.*

MA. What's this?

KAT. Guess.

> MA *sniffs her soup.*

> She'll get it.

MA. Fennel. Is it?

MAUDIE. Yeah yeah yeah.

KAT. Better than a bloodhound.

> KAT *eats.*

> Go on, then.

MA. In a minute.

KAT. Weird, though.

MA. What?

KAT. Weird taste.

MA. I love it.

KAT. That's why she made it.

MA/MAUDIE. Yes. / Yeah.

KAT. But truthfully it's like eating an old river or something. A bowlful of Thames, complete with all the shit.

MA. Kat!

KAT. Sorry.

MA. There are plenty of other words.

KAT. Good to see you up again. Isn't it, Maudie?

MAUDIE. Excellent, truly.

KAT. Have a spoonful. Go on.

MA has a spoonful of soup.

Does this little dance in your mouth, doesn't it? Am I savoury, am I sweet?

MA. Actually it does.

KAT (*to* MAUDIE). Do the dance, do the Fennel Dance, go on. Savoury or sweet?

MAUDIE *does a shuffle.*

MA. What's this in aid of?

MAUDIE (*dancing, croons*). Savoury.

KAT. You stirring your stumps again.

MAUDIE (*dancing, croons*). Savoury savoury.

KAT. Welcome back to the land of the living, Ma! (*To* MAUDIE.) We missed you, didn't we?

MAUDIE (*dancing, croons*). Sweet!

KAT. Enough. Back.

MAUDIE *stands behind* MA.

KAT *eats.*

MA *watches* KAT.

You're not eating.

MA. Look at you.

KAT. What?

MA. You're different.

KAT. No, I'm not. Am I?

MA. You're.

KAT. What?

MA. I don't know. You're ample.

KAT. Ample?

MA. Inside, I mean.

KAT. Ample?

MA. Don't get all –

KAT. I'm not –

MA. A house of many rooms. You're an oak tree with many perches.

KAT. Alright, Mrs Wordsworth. Now if you'd kindly eat your soup.

MA. I can't.

KAT. You've got to eat.

MA. Got to?

KAT. I didn't mean –

MA. I haven't got to anything, Katherine.

KAT. No.

MA. Got to.

KAT. Sorry.

KAT *eats*.

MA *watches her*.

MA. If you'd been as ill as I have, you wouldn't have an appetite either.

KAT. I know, you're thin as a string, I could twang you.

MA. Twang me?

KAT. That was a joke. Ho ho?

MA. Funny sort of joke.

MAUDIE. Ho ho.

KAT. Course I'd never twang you.

MA. No, you wouldn't. You wouldn't dare.

KAT. No.

KAT *eats*.

MA. Where d'you get the fennel, then?

KAT. She dug it up.

MA. *My* fennel?

MAUDIE. Kat said to.

KAT. As a treat for you.

MAUDIE. Yeah yeah yeah.

MA. I see.

KAT. There's another bulb out there, Ma.

MA. One?

KAT. One or two.

MA. Which?

MAUDIE. One.

KAT. Quiet.

MA. Prevaricator. Better eat my soup then. Seeing it's the penultimate bulb.

   MA *has a spoonful*.

   They watch her.

KAT. And?

MA. I've had better.

KAT (*to* MAUDIE). Bread.

MAUDIE (*bringing bread*). The body, the life, alive alive-o.

KAT. Did I say talk?

MAUDIE. No.

   MAUDIE *resumes her place.*

KAT. Guess who come in the yard yesterday.

MA. Who?

KAT. Guess.

MA. I don't know, do I? I've been rotting here for weeks.

KAT. Hodge.

MA. Jack Hodge?

KAT. Black Jack Hodge.

MA. In our yard?

KAT. Strolls in like he's just passing. Don't see me, I'm on the turn of the stairs.

MA. And?

KAT. He just stands looking.

MA. And?

KAT. All the cars gleaming, the boys in their beautiful soft dark suits.

MA. And?

KAT. I watched his face turn sour.

MA *chuckles*.

I know why he came, too.

MA. Why?

KAT. He'd just heard I got Greening's.

MA. What?

KAT. Yup.

MA. You did?

KAT. Yup.

MA. Kitty Kat.

KAT. I got 'em, Ma. They're coming over to us.

MA. You clever puss!

KAT. I got Greening's!

MA. Oh, she's a sly one, isn't she, Maudie?

MAUDIE. Sly as a fox in a box.

MA. You got Greening's. *You* did.

KAT. Greening's, White's, Fuller's, they've all come over to us now –

MA. Not Enright's.

KAT. I'm working on Enright's.

MA. Are you?

KAT. We get Enright's, he's done for.

MA. Black Jack Hodge.

MAUDIE. Bom bom bom.

MA. Mean as a cornered rat, that man. But now finally. When I'm back, I'll.

KAT *and* MA *look at each other*.

I'm coming back.

KAT *eats*.

I'm getting my strength back. More every day. Aren't I, Maudie?

MAUDIE. Stronger than Superman.

MA. I will be there. There's no question – what now, when he finally? No. Not all the years I've been working and waiting and watching that lump of – decades! I will be there to remind him how he jeered and smeared our name and spat on my stairs and swaggered across my yard and now *finally* – no! No! I will be…

MA *pants*.

KAT *waits till her breathing calms*.

KAT. What did the doctor say?

MA. Leech.

KAT. I thought you liked Doc McBride.

MA. Quack.

MAUDIE. Duck McBride.

MA. Ha! I want a second opinion.

KAT. You've been seriously ill.

MA. I'm better now.

KAT. Still breathless. Still very pale.

MAUDIE. Grey.

KAT. Isn't she?

MAUDIE. Face like porridge.

KAT. All those nights of fever.

MAUDIE. Slippery wet.

KAT. Your breath.

MAUDIE. Rattling in and rattling out.

KAT. It was frightening.

MAUDIE. Whooh!

KAT. And you'd only just got over the cheese thing.

MA. That was her fault!

MAUDIE. No no no.

KAT. How d'you work that out?

MA. Don't defend her.

KAT. Maudie was locked in her hole at the time.

MAUDIE. Banged up in my cubbyhole, click, scrape, Kat's got the key.

KAT. How was the cheese thing her fault?

MA. I can't eat the nameless messes she puts in front of me.

KAT. But you can't have cheese, we all know that. Cheese is catastrophic. Isn't it?

MA. Alright!

KAT. So what made you do it?

MA. I told you. I was peckish.

KAT. Peckish?

MA. In the night.

KAT. You ate a wheel of Stilton.

MA. I –

KAT. Six pounds of cheese! We thought we'd been raided by monstrous mice.

MA. There's no need to get descriptive.

KAT. But no, it was Ma, a woman unable to eat pressed curds of any kind –

MAUDIE. Not even the one with holes.

MA. Oh, the one with holes!

KAT. You gorged like a mad maggot who thinks it's the End of Days and then –

MA. Don't.

KAT. Great cranks of pain, heartburn, starts in your chest, up your arms, like a heart attack, you double over, migraine drills your head, the light sears your eyes though your room's darker than the blessed well, then vomiting –

MAUDIE. Supersize. Green bile, brown bile –

KAT. Blood.

MAUDIE. You were epic, Mrs G.

KAT. And then you get the infection. You've really been through it, Ma.

MA *sighs a deep sigh.*

What did the doctor say this morning?

MA. As if you didn't talk to him.

KAT. He told me you'd strained your heart.

MA. He listened to it.

KAT (*under her breath*). Did well to find it.

MA. What?

KAT. He told me one more infection could be fatal.

MA. Fatal?

MAUDIE. End of Days.

MA. He didn't say fatal. Did he?

KAT. Sorry.

MA. He didn't say it to me. He said to rest.

KAT. Total rest, yup.

MA. Fatal?

KAT. Sorry. I shouldn't have said.

Silence.

MA *stirs her soup.*

KAT *gets two bottles of pills from her pocket and puts them on the table.*

MA (*quiet*). What's this?

KAT. One for your heart, one for your chest. Every four hours. Maudie will do it.

MA. What?

MAUDIE. Maudie will?

MA. You'll do it.

KAT. I can't.

MA. You will.

KAT. You're not thinking straight.

MA. Don't tell me what I'm thinking. You will do it.

KAT. You want us to see off Hodge?

MA. I want to finish Hodge.

MAUDIE. Bom bom –

KAT/MA. Quiet!

KAT. Then I need to be on the spot, sleep at the yard. Maudie'll have to look after you.

MA *pulls* KAT *close.*

MA (*quiet*). You'd leave me alone with her roaming the house at will like a – like a person?

KAT (*quiet*). What choice have we got?

MA (*quiet*). She's never been unlocked at night before.

KAT (*quiet*). I know.

MA (*quiet*). Creeping round getting ready to – I won't have it! (*Normal volume.*) I'll doctor myself.

KAT. Total rest, he says.

MAUDIE. Yeah.

KAT. Time to stop, he says, or –

MAUDIE. Yeah yeah yeah.

MA. But Hodge!

KAT. I'll do it.

MA. You need to be sharp to finish that man. Fast as a bright new silver knife.

KAT. Don't think I can do it?

MA. No!

They look at each other.

He's mine.

KAT. He was.

MA. I should be there, at least!

KAT. But you're too weak to lift your spoon. Sadly. I'll tell you the story when I'm back. Promise. Every blood-red detail.

MA. I don't want the story!

KAT (*to* MAUDIE). Clear the table.

MAUDIE *clears the table.*

And bring the ledger. It's Settling Day.

MAUDIE *goes.*

KAT *unlocks the strongbox, gets out banknotes, pound coins, a pair of pliers.*

She puts them on the table, neat and separate.

MAUDIE *comes with a ledger.*

The rusty old dusty old ledger. (*To* MAUDIE, *as she moves away.*) Stay.

MAUDIE *stands still.*

MA *stirs herself.*

MA. Is it Settling Day? Already?

KAT. The world rolled on while you were on your sickbed. Come on, this'll cheer you up.

MA. She gets the shakes on Settling Day. Look at her.

KAT. She's always got the shakes.

MA. Yes, you're quiet now you're for it. Read out her Misdemeanours. You listening?

MAUDIE *nods.*

KAT (*reading*). Honestly, Ma.

MA. What?

KAT. I can hardly read your writing any more.

MA. I've been ill. I've had pneumonia.

KAT. This was before. Like a little spider weaving through the columns, a just-before-winter spider, she's dragged her legs through the ink and here she is, weaving down the page.

MA. You're in a strange mood.

KAT. Am I?

MA. Read them out.

KAT (*reads*). Misdemeanours: mud everywhere. She's lost my pink silk blouse. Bath-stain remains. Asleep in kitchen. Cold lumpy porridge. Complained she was tired. Rubbery chicken, couldn't chew through it. (*To* MA.) I remember that chicken.

MA. It set off my tooth again.

KAT (*reads*). Demanded a blanket. Bloody lamb chop. Told me Kat had taken my blouse to dry cleaner's. Ironing not finished. Found my blouse in her cubbyhole, dirty and torn.

MA. That blouse was my mother's, she's ruined it.

MAUDIE. I'm truly sorry –

MA. You're always sorry after.

MAUDIE. The old pink was thin, Mrs G, she didn't want to go in the wash –

MA. You lied to my face like a street-corner tart.

KAT. So. Deductions or Pliers? Ma?

MA. Pliers.

MAUDIE. No!

KAT. How else you going to learn? I don't make the rules.

MA. You do.

KAT (*laughing*). I do!

MA. Beautiful rules you made for her.

KAT. Thanks, Ma.

    KAT *picks up the pliers*.

MAUDIE. Not Pliers. Please, please, I can't!

KAT. It's your own fault.

MAUDIE. Yeah yeah yeah.

KAT. Lying's against the rules, you know that.

MAUDIE. I'm sorry.

KAT. What can I do, Maudie?

MAUDIE. Be merciful.

    KAT *contemplates* MAUDIE.

    KAT *kicks out her chair*.

KAT. Sit.

    MAUDIE *shakes her head*.

    Sit.

MAUDIE. I can't bear the pain.

MA. You will, though.

MAUDIE. Not again.

KAT. Sit or you'll make things worse for yourself.

MAUDIE *sits*.

Open.

MAUDIE *opens her mouth*.

MAUDIE *bolts to the door*.

MA. Stop her.

MAUDIE *opens the door*.

Sunlight streams through it.

Stop her! Kat!

KAT. Go on, then. Who's making you stay?

MAUDIE *hesitates on the threshold*.

Go back to it, go on! Out in the air, nowhere safe to sleep,
always sleeping in snatches, under bridges and bushes,
questions round and round your head all night, will they find
me and do something, when will they, what will they do it
with, what will they do? Walking and walking, hungry and
stinking itching dirty, nowhere to wash have a piss stash
your stuff, nowhere safe, hooking up with some guy just to
lie in his rank arms and feel a bit safe for the night, his foul
breath on your face for the night, sent out begging for him
for his crack, remember the lump of cruelty I found you
with? Black sides you had, black thoughts, and the looks you
got, remember those guys in suits who stamped on your feet?

MAUDIE. No need for that.

KAT. The room in the hostel you were too scared to stay in,
remember? Ex-cons, addicts, paedos and Maudie, the
cared-for child? Go on, then.

Silence.

MAUDIE *shuts the door*.

She sits down and opens her mouth.

Beg.

MAUDIE *bows her head, puts her hands together.*

Harder.

MAUDIE *slides to the floor and prostrates herself. Then she crawls towards* KAT, *who keeps backing away.*

Say things.

MAUDIE. Kat, Miss Kat, Miss Katherine, I swear to you no lies, never ever no more, no whining, no moaning, I'll work and work and sing if you keep me safe, if you let my teeth stay in my head like the little white fish in the cave, please save me out of your supersize kindness, see? There's me swimming into your heart and look at the size of it, it's a McPalace of Mercy –

KAT *laughs delightedly and puts down the pliers.*

MA. Now what?

KAT. I get such a kick out of this!

MA. Get on with it.

KAT (*rubbing her chest*). Such a lovely warm feel in here. Ooh. It's a little bit sexy, too.

MA. Katherine!

KAT. What?

MA. Disgusting.

KAT. Is it?

MA. No one wants to hear that. Things are private for a reason.

KAT. Sorry. I didn't mean –

MA. Disgusting.

KAT. I said sorry.

MA. Very well. We'll draw a veil.

KAT *picks up the pliers.*

KAT. Up.

MAUDIE *gets up slowly*.

We'll have Deductions instead.

MA. What?

MAUDIE. God bless you.

MA. I want Pliers.

KAT. My rules.

MA. But –

KAT. Beautiful rules, you said.

MA. I want spitting and sobbing and splinters of bone.

KAT. When she begged so nicely?

MA. Yes.

KAT. Sorry. Not today.

MAUDIE *takes* KAT*'s hand and kisses it*.

MAUDIE. Blessings fall on your bare head and run down your face like the rain.

KAT. Enough.

KAT *puts the pliers back in the strongbox*.

MAUDIE. The destination of this bus has changed.

KAT. Come here.

MAUDIE *goes to stand by* KAT, *who is writing in the ledger*.

I'm taking five pounds a month over the next twenty months for Mrs G's blouse. Plus a pound interest. I've scheduled your debt here, see? Oh, what's the point? But it's written down. And I'm taking six pounds for Misdemeanours. So that's twenty-four pounds this month. (*To* MA.) Alright?

MA *shrugs*.

Let's have your 'M'.

MAUDIE *writes M in the ledger*.

KAT *counts out twenty-four pounds.*

MAUDIE *stows her cash in her purse.*

KAT *puts the purse back in the strongbox, locks it.*

Safe in the bank of Kat. What d'you say?

MAUDIE. Thank you.

KAT *waits.*

Thanks very much, very excellent, truly.

KAT. Cos remember where I found you.

MAUDIE. Yeah yeah yeah.

KAT. Say it.

MAUDIE. Down by the river. In the dark, in the dirt.

KAT. You were nothing, really. I could've took a deep breath and blown you away, like a dandelion. Now look: clean, sober, ninety-eight pounds in the strongbox.

MAUDIE. My own cubbyhole.

KAT. Yup.

MAUDIE. Company.

KAT. Yup.

MAUDIE. You crossed the road for me.

KAT. I did.

MAUDIE. Jackpot.

KAT *closes the ledger.*

MA. What about me?

KAT. What?

MA. What can I have?

KAT. How d'you mean?

MA. I'm not allowed Pliers or cheese or Jack Hodge – what can I have? I want something.

KAT. Like what?

MA. I don't know. Something! Here, here, in here – (*Rubbing her chest*.) it's empty.

KAT. You're hungry.

MA. This is different, it's like a, like a great black cave that could swallow the sea and eat mountains and –

MAUDIE. Giant McCavern.

MA. Yes!

KAT. Eat something, then!

> MA *grabs the paring knife*.

> KAT *and* MAUDIE *back off instantly*.

> MA *stabs it into the table*.

MA. Oh, we're topdog now. This is it, Maudie, this is what we've been waiting for. Kat's the dog!

MAUDIE. Bow-wow!

MA. She's seen the edge and it's got her blood up. I can feel you!

KAT. What?

MA. Setting your shoulder to the stone, see if you can heave me over. Look at the drop – that should shatter her. Heave! You want to peek over the edge and see my brains seeping out of my skull down there, don't you?

MAUDIE. Grey goo out of your ears.

KAT. No.

MA. Liar! What happens to liars' tongues?

KAT/MAUDIE. They shrivel in their heads.

> MA *closes her eyes in exhaustion*.

MA. I should be proud, shouldn't I? to have mothered an Amazon. Send you off with a bursting heart.

KAT. It's time, Ma.

MA. But I feel sick to my stomach.

KAT. You got up too soon, that's all.

MAUDIE. Whoops!

MA. I'm tired.

KAT. Rest.

MA. So tired, Kat. All I want is sleep.

KAT. Rest and Maudie will see to you. Don't look like that,
    Maudie loves you, don't you?

MAUDIE. Course I do, Mrs G.

MA. I don't like it.

KAT. It's what I got her for.

MA. Doesn't mean I have to like it.

    KAT *hands* MAUDIE *the pills*.

KAT. You're to sleep up here.

MAUDIE. Yeah?

KAT. You look after Mrs G like she was your own ma.

MAUDIE. Better than her.

KAT. Alright. And if any harm comes to her –

MAUDIE. No no no!

KAT. What will happen?

MAUDIE. No harm, no need for alarm.

KAT. What happened to the old housekeeper?

MAUDIE. Don't say it.

KAT. Say it.

    MAUDIE *shakes her head*.

    KAT *takes hold of* MAUDIE*'s jaw*.

MAUDIE. It rained and rained and the well filled up and up.
    And.

KAT. Say.

MAUDIE. She couldn't.

KAT. No. And if anything happens while I'm away, I'll tie you down in the well like Bromwich. No one will hear you down there. And we'll just wait for rain. It's been a wet spring this year, hasn't it?

MAUDIE. Cats and dogs.

KAT. I'll do it, Maudie.

MAUDIE. I know you will.

KAT. So don't let me down.

MAUDIE. Never ever.

KAT (*to* MA). Happy?

> MA *shrugs*.

> KAT *stretches her whole body and then shakes herself*.

Right. That's the plan. Coat.

> MAUDIE *helps* KAT *into her coat*.

> KAT *picks up her apple, throws it high, catches and pockets it*.

> KAT *picks up the strongbox*.

(*To* MAUDIE.) Work hard. (*To* MA.) Rest.

> KAT *opens the door*.

MA. Kiss me.

KAT. What did you say?

MA. One kiss?

KAT (*not moving*). I must get to the yard. Get Hodge.

MA. Warm on the cheek.

KAT. I must run.

MA. Kat?

> KAT *stares at* MA.

> KAT *shuts and locks the door from the outside*.

She goes.

Silence.

Better get your things.

MAUDIE. Seats are available on the upper deck.

MAUDIE goes.

MA forces herself up to walk unsteadily, slowly.

MA. Come on. You're not done yet.

MA sits, exhausted.

Fatal?

MA closes her eyes and instantly falls asleep.

MAUDIE comes with a dog bed, which she puts down.

She watches MA.

She puts MA's apple in her apron pocket.

She pulls the paring knife out of the table.

MA startles.

MAUDIE pockets the knife.

What?

MAUDIE. Mrs G?

MA. What you doing?

MAUDIE points to the dog bed.

Oh. Yes. Foot of the bed.

MAUDIE puts the dog bed at the foot of the bed.

Colin used to sleep there. You can be there.

MAUDIE. Jackpot.

MAUDIE and MA look at each other.

MA. I'll do my hair first. Get my things.

MAUDIE gets a hand-mirror, hairbrush and moisturiser.

MA *takes the hairbrush.*

Oh, you do it.

MAUDIE *brushes* MA*'s hair from behind.*

MAUDIE. This?

MA. Harder. Yes. I brushed your hair once.

MAUDIE. You?

MA. Scrubbed you clean.

MAUDIE. When?

MA. When you came. I cut all your hair off. It had to be cut, it was stiff with muck. And the nails on your feet were like claws. You sat in the bath and cried while I clipped them off.

MAUDIE. Was I – ?

MA. Oh, disgusting. Shivering, sweating, whining. Spitting sometimes. And the language.

MAUDIE. Mucky?

MA. Don't you remember?

MAUDIE. Was I mental?

MA. Probably.

MAUDIE. Why, though?

MA. Drink. And a dirty life.

MAUDIE. Mm.

MA. Best to forget all the things you've been. We'll draw a veil.

MAUDIE. Abracadabra.

MA *peers into the hand-mirror.*

MA. I'm all bones now.

MAUDIE. How many?

MA. What, all together? Two hundred and six, isn't it?

MAUDIE. Whooh!

MA. Something like that. And the wind'll blow through them all.

MAUDIE *blows gently on the back of* MA*'s neck.*

MA *shivers.*

MAUDIE *touches the bones in* MA*'s neck.*

(*Startled.*) Don't!

MAUDIE. Hurts?

MA. What you doing? Come round here where I can see you.

MAUDIE *comes in front of her, offering her the moisturiser.*

MA *grabs it.*

That's mine. And the hairbrush.

MAUDIE *holds out the hairbrush.*

(*Grabbing it.*) Mine! Everything you can see's mine. What are you up to?

MAUDIE *shakes her head.*

Something. I won't have it!

MAUDIE. Aye aye, Captain.

MA (*shivering*). I'm cold.

MAUDIE. Bed?

MA. Get the trunk, there's a rug in there.

MA *shivers uncontrollably.*

MAUDIE *pulls a trunk from under the bed and opens it.*

I couldn't get warm last night. Not for a minute. I don't think I slept all night and all I wanted was sleep. Put it on me.

MA *stands.*

MAUDIE *puts the rug round* MA.

Do you love me, Maudie?

MAUDIE. Course I do, Mrs G.

MA. Rub my back. Get me warm.

MAUDIE *rubs* MA*'s back.*

MAUDIE. Like the nipper.

MA. Who?

MAUDIE. Couldn't never get warm after his bath.

MA. Yours?

MAUDIE. No.

MA. Well, who was he?

MAUDIE. Frankie. You're better in bed.

MA. It's freezing in there. Like a fish packed in ice.

MAUDIE. We'd give him a good hard rub, then a cuddle.

MA. That's it!

MAUDIE. Enough?

MA. A cuddle. Hold me.

MAUDIE *stares.*

MAUDIE *hesitates, then shakes her head.*

I'll give you more.

MAUDIE. More?

MA. Money. Extra.

MAUDIE *considers* MA.

We'll write it down. Shall we?

MAUDIE. Alright.

MA. Put your arms round me.

MAUDIE *hugs* MA.

Silence.

You're warm. Oh!

MAUDIE. Mm.

MA. I'd forgotten this.

MAUDIE. And me.

MA. Nice.

MAUDIE. Yeah.

> MAUDIE *rocks* MA *slightly as she sings.*

> (*Croons softly.*) Dem bones dem bones dem dry bones, dem bones dem bones dem dry bones, dem bones dem bones dem dry bones, now hear the word of the Lord!

MA. It hurts behind my breastbone.

MAUDIE. Yeah?

MA. Indigestion?

MAUDIE. Giant McCavern.

MA. Come back, has he?

MAUDIE. Don't stay away long.

MA. You feel him?

MAUDIE. Always.

> MA *sits.*

> MAUDIE *opens the moisturiser, hands it to* MA *and holds up the mirror for her.*

> MA *dabs moisturiser on her face.*

MA. Giant McCavern.

MAUDIE. Mm.

MA. Deep as the sea, isn't he?

MAUDIE. I don't know the sea.

MA. You've never seen the sea?

MAUDIE. Seen the river.

MA. Oh, the sea's deeper, wider, blue, sometimes green and fierce and – you've never seen waves! They come curling, they never stop, and the air smells of – I don't know, but it does you good.

MAUDIE. Not like the river, then.

MA. Filthy brown.

MAUDIE. And the mud.

MA. What does the river smell of?

MAUDIE. Bad days.

MA. How long were you down there?

MAUDIE. They're gone now. I'm here now.

MA. That's what came squeezing out of your skin. And your breath. Pestilential.

MAUDIE. Eh?

MA. Foul.

MAUDIE. Something I can do you for the pain, Mrs G.

MA. You can?

MAUDIE. Yeah.

MA. Do it.

MAUDIE. It's Extra.

They look at each other.

MA. Do it.

MAUDIE. Write it down, will we? Before.

MA. Very well.

MAUDIE *gets the ledger and gives it to* MA.

MAUDIE. All the cockles alive alive-o.

MA. Nothing's changed between us. Is that fully understood?

MAUDIE. Aye aye, Captain.

MA (*writing*). I'll do a new column. X is for Extra.

MAUDIE. Excellent, truly. (*Over* MA*'s shoulder.*) And one for Hold from before.

MA. Written down.

MAUDIE. All the mussels winking and blinking.

MA. Now then.

>   MAUDIE *pulls up the trunk and sits.*

>   *She takes* MA*'s feet into her lap and massages them with moisturiser.*

>   Oh. Oh. Oh, Maudie!

MAUDIE. True thing. (*Sings.*) Your hip bone connected to your back bone, back bone connected to your neck bone, neck bone connected to your head bone, now hear the word of the Lord!

MA. Oh my.

MAUDIE. Here's a piece.

MA. Of what?

MAUDIE. There's all of us in her bed, Spiderman's on the pillows, then there's Netta, Frankie and me, all tangled up, arms and legs and backs. All quiet. Safe.

MA. That it?

MAUDIE. It's everything.

MA. Netta?

MAUDIE. Frankie's ma.

MA. What was she to you?

MAUDIE. The girl inside the girl inside the girl.

MA. Cryptic. We had a bed. Cotton sheets, crisp, cool in summer. Cold in winter, king-size, no need to touch, not even toes, Mr G a tiny bald figure on the far white edge.

MAUDIE. There's a Mr G?

MA. There was.

MAUDIE. Run away, did he?

MA. Dropped dead one morning. (*Intense pleasure from her feet.*) Oh!

MAUDIE. How's Old McCavern now?

MA (*realising*). Gone. You're a witch, Maudie.

MAUDIE (*softly*). Abracadabra.

MA closes her eyes and falls instantly asleep.

Singing softly, keeping an eye on MA, MAUDIE *looks in the trunk.*

She takes out a dress.

She takes off her apron, puts it out of MA*'s reach.*

She puts the dress on over her leggings and T-shirt.

(*Croons softly during this.*) Dem bones dem bones gonna walk around, dem bones dem bones gonna walk around, dem bones dem bones gonna walk around, dem bones dem bones gonna walk around... (*Etc.*)

MA startles awake.

MA. That's Kat's.

MAUDIE *freezes.*

She was skinny once, too. Take off the cap.

MAUDIE *shakes her head.*

I know you're devoted to it for some obscure reason. Just for a moment.

MAUDIE *reluctantly takes off her McDonald's cap.*

Turn round. Slowly.

MAUDIE *turns, watching* MA.

MAUDIE. You're looking at me.

MA. What?

MAUDIE. Aren't you?

MA. Of course I am.

MAUDIE. First time you ever truly looked at me.

MA hands MAUDIE *the mirror.*

MAUDIE *looks at herself.*

MA. Well?

MAUDIE *hands it back.*

MAUDIE. Thought it was going to be someone else.

MAUDIE *puts her cap back on and puts the apron on over the dress.*

MA. She was a kitten once.

MAUDIE. Who?

MA. Kat.

MAUDIE. No.

MA. A long time ago.

MAUDIE. She was an egg.

MA. Oho!

MAUDIE. Crawls out, licks up the goo, slides off.

MA. She is hard.

MAUDIE. Diamond.

MA. Harder than before.

MAUDIE. Will she do your feet?

MA. No.

MAUDIE. Sing to you?

MA. No.

MAUDIE. Will she hold you?

Silence.

She won't.

MA. If you do and do and do and do to someone. Can it be undone?

MAUDIE. No.

MA. Then what's left?

MAUDIE. There's others.

MA (*blankly*). Who?

MAUDIE. Do you love me, Mrs G?

MA. Extraordinary question.

MAUDIE *brings the knife out of her apron.*

MA *puts up her hands.*

You sharpen it?

MAUDIE. Yesterday.

MA. On the back step, like I told you?

MAUDIE. Aye aye, Captain. It's wicked.

MA. How will you do it?

MAUDIE. Cut your throat's quickest.

MA. Yes.

MAUDIE *pulls the apple out of her apron.*

She slices the apple in half.

MAUDIE. That *is* sharp. Peckish?

MA. Not really.

MAUDIE *stabs half and proffers it to* MA.

MAUDIE. Take, eat, the body and the life.

MA *takes the half-apple.*

They eat, watching each other.

MAUDIE *taps the knife on her knee.*

MA. Do you hate me, Maudie?

MAUDIE. Course I do, Mrs G.

MA. If you kill me –

MAUDIE. If?

MA. You'll have to run before Kat comes back.

MAUDIE *nods.*

Out on your own again.

MAUDIE. Not. No. I'd be with my street family.

MA. Family.

MAUDIE. What?

MA. They're not family. Family stick together.

MAUDIE. We stick.

MA. Where are they, then? Did they come knocking for you, asking? No one knows where you are, no one cares.

MAUDIE. Netta cares.

MA. She's not coming, though. Is she? Your family are here.

MAUDIE *spits out pips*.

MAUDIE. Might not do you in. Might just leave. Kat's off at the yard, isn't she? Gone for days. You're here, hungry, lonely, too weak to help yourself.

MA. I'd ring her up!

MAUDIE. Would she answer? There's a worry. Would she come? There's another, blinking at the bottom of the bucket. Might leave you to wither away. Harder now, isn't she?

MA. You could never come back.

MAUDIE. Good riddance.

MA. The warm, the food in the freezer, the Extras you can earn looking after me, the company –

MAUDIE. You?!

MA. What d'you want?

MAUDIE. I dunno yet.

MAUDIE *puts the knife in her apron*.

MA *starts to shiver*.

You cold?

MA *nods*.

MAUDIE *touches her hands*.

You're freezing up. Come on.

MAUDIE *helps her up and over to the bed.*

MA *shakes her head.*

What?

MA. Hold me first. I know. It's Extra. Please?

MA *puts her arms round* MAUDIE.

MAUDIE. What's up?

MA. I'm scared.

MAUDIE. What of?

MA. It's my deathbed. I know it is.

MAUDIE. You need to sleep, Mrs G.

MA. What if I don't wake up again?

MAUDIE. Then you'll be free.

MAUDIE *strokes* MA*'s hair.*

MA. I've not been scared since I was a child.

MAUDIE (*tucking* MA *into bed*). It tires you out. Sometimes it gets so big you think you'll burst to bits. But sometimes you go out the other side of it, and it's all quiet there, like flying over the dark. With your cape swirling out behind you. Epic.

MA. That pain. You feel it, too?

MAUDIE. Always.

MA. Netta?

MAUDIE. Netta. Frankie. A thousand thousand things beating about in there. What if I lay along your back and keep you warm, think you'd sleep then?

MA. Maybe.

MAUDIE. It's Extra.

MA. Excellent.

MAUDIE *gets her own blanket from the dog bed and settles along* MA*'s back.*

MAUDIE. Did Colin lie like this?

MA. If I let him.

MAUDIE. After Mr G, was he?

MA. Long after.

MAUDIE. Was he a good lover?

MA. He was a sheepdog.

> MAUDIE *laughs*.

> That went right through me.

> *They laugh*.

MAUDIE. Better?

MA. Mm.

MAUDIE (*sings softly*). Dem bones dem bones dem dry bones, dem bones dem bones dem dry bones, dem bones dem bones dem dry bones, now hear the word of the Lord!

TWO

The table is set with silverware, candles lit. KAT *wheels in* MA *in a wheelchair.*

KAT. A toast?

MA. Of course!

> KAT *pulls a bottle of vodka from her coat pocket.*

KAT. Should you?

MA. Certainly.

> KAT *pours two shots.*

KAT. Jack Hodge, finally –

MA. Finally!

KAT. Finished and done for!

MA. Jack Hodge, skewered and skinned!

> *They drink.*

KAT. Pleased with me?

MA. Very.

KAT. Proud of me?

MA. Very.

KAT. Jealous?

> KAT *laughs, takes off her coat, stretches her body and shakes herself.*

MA. Strangely not.

KAT. What?

MA. Jealous. It all seems very far away.

KAT. How d'you mean?

MA. You hungry?

KAT. Starving. Feel like I haven't eaten for days.

MA. Excellent. We want to feast you. Maudie's killed a chicken and picked the apples. She's been working in that kitchen like a slave. Here she is!

MAUDIE *pushes on a trolley with pots.*

She wears KAT*'s dress under her apron and cap.*

MAUDIE (*removing and replacing lids*). Voilà! Fennel soup! Chicken stew –

MA. With fennel.

MAUDIE. Mash and fennel! Alphabetti Spaghetti –

KAT. With –?

MAUDIE. Don't be daft. And afters is apples baked in cider.

MA. We had to get extra fennel.

KAT. I don't even like it.

MA/MAUDIE. It's your favourite! Voilà!

KAT. What's happened here?

MA. What d'you mean?

KAT. I don't know. Something's happened. Something's going on.

KAT *looks from one to the other.*

Is that my dress?

MAUDIE. No.

MA. Ah.

MAUDIE. It's mine.

KAT. She's wearing my dress.

MA. You hardly wore it. You didn't like it.

KAT. How did she come by it?

MAUDIE. Fair and square.

MA. You can't get into it, anyway.

KAT. What?

MA. The mighty oak! Too ample! Too many rooms!

KAT. How did she get it, Ma?

MAUDIE. Swapsies.

MA. Yes yes yes.

KAT. You gave her my dress?

MA. Gave her! She worked for it fair and square. Now don't get
squeaky, Kat. Let's eat.

KAT. What are Swapsies?

MA. Right, well. Extras can be swapped for certain things –

KAT. My dress?

MAUDIE. My dress.

KAT. Did I say you could talk?

MAUDIE. No. But I got it fair and square.

MA. Sssh, Maudie, I'll do this.

KAT. Are you protecting her?

MA. Just –

KAT. What are Extras?

MA. We've kept a strict tally.

KAT. We?

MA. Maudie and me.

KAT. She can't read, she can't write.

MA. Her letters now she can.

MAUDIE. She shown me.

KAT. Fetch the ledger.

MAUDIE *goes.*

MA. Kat.

KAT. Ma?

MA. Are you angry?

KAT. No.

MA. You sure? These days I find I don't know what I'm feeling half the time.

MAUDIE *comes with the ledger.*

KAT *opens it.*

KAT. There's a new column.

MAUDIE. X.

MA. For Extra.

MAUDIE/MA. Excellent.

They laugh.

MA. We agreed, Maudie and me.

KAT *puts the ledger on the table.*

KAT. Explain.

MAUDIE. H is for Hold.

KAT. And S?

MAUDIE. Is for Sleep and F is for Feet.

KAT. How much?

MAUDIE. A pound.

KAT. Per Extra?

MA. We agreed, Maudie and me.

KAT. I see. And over here. Under Misdemeanours.

MA. What?

KAT. Nothing. Nada. Zilch.

MAUDIE. Mm.

MA. That's good, isn't it?

KAT. All this time and not a single Misdemeanour?

MA. Commendable.

KAT. Improbable.

MA. She's an example.

KAT. A bloody miracle.

MAUDIE. Let's shout and sing!

> MA *laughs*.

> KAT *starts totting up*.

MA. I'm sleeping like a child. I'm getting lighter, Kat. Aren't you pleased?

KAT. Ecstatic.

MA. You don't look it.

KAT. Ninety-four pounds.

> MA *and* MAUDIE *gasp*.

> Thirty pounds wages, sixty-four pounds Extras. Less five pounds repayment, eighty-nine.

MAUDIE. Mine?

MA. It does seem a lot. But you can't take it with you.

KAT. I won't be. Or I wouldn't be if I paid it.

MA. Now, Kat –

KAT. I don't know what's been going on, but I know when I'm being ripped off. I'm not paying that out.

> *Silence*.

MAUDIE. Mrs G?

MA. We agreed.

KAT. Not me.

MA. Maudie and I agreed in good faith and we wrote it down.

KAT. I was working day and night to get you what you wanted.

MA. I'm proud of you.

KAT. Working my arse off.

MAUDIE (*under her breath*). It's still on.

KAT. While back at the ranch, every penny I make's running out the door.

MAUDIE. Eighty-nine pounds, Mrs G.

MA. Yes.

KAT. No.

MAUDIE. Stroke your feet, stroke your hair, fair and square.

MA. I know, yes.

KAT. No.

MAUDIE. She's taking advantage.

KAT. *I* am?

MAUDIE. It's only right.

KAT. You think you decide what's right here?

MAUDIE *goes to the door and opens it.*

A sunset light comes through.

MA. Stop her.

MAUDIE *stands on the threshold.*

KAT. She's not going anywhere. She's got too much to lose. She's working the seam, that's all.

MAUDIE. Goodbye, Mrs G.

MA. Pay her.

MAUDIE. I'll think of you sometimes.

MA. Please.

KAT. Let her go.

MA. I need her.

KAT. I can get you another one.

MA. Kat.

KAT. I'll just wait till dark and drive down to the river.

MA (*realising*). I don't want another one.

KAT. There's loads to choose from.

MA. I want Maudie. Maudie!

> MA *holds out her arms to* MAUDIE.
>
> MAUDIE *looks at* MA, *then at* KAT.
>
> KAT *unlocks the strongbox and counts eighty-nine pounds onto the table.*
>
> MAUDIE *closes the door and picks up her money.*

MAUDIE. Thank you.

KAT. No, thank *you*.

MAUDIE. No, thank *you*, very excellent, yeah, cos where would I be else? You could've took a breath and blown me to dust, and look at me now.

KAT. I'm looking.

MAUDIE. Truly.

KAT. You think everything's changed so much that I can't make you sorry.

MAUDIE. No. Because you can.

KAT. That's right.

MA. Good. Let's eat.

> KAT *picks up the vodka bottle.*

MAUDIE. How much for a shot?

KAT. Of vodka?

MAUDIE. Vloddy vod.

MA. No.

MAUDIE. How much?

MA. She shouldn't have it, Kat.

KAT. Twenty pounds.

MAUDIE. Steep.

KAT. Isn't it?

MAUDIE *puts a twenty-pound note on the table.*

MA. Don't let her have it.

KAT *pours a shot.*

You don't want it, Maudie.

MAUDIE. I do.

MA. You don't want to go back to that terrible –

MAUDIE *drinks.*

MAUDIE. Vladivostok!

KAT *laughs.*

She pours two shots and hands one to MA.

She and MA *drink.*

(*Sings.*) Three three, the rivals! Two two, the lily-white boys, clothèd all in green –

KAT/MAUDIE (*sing*). Ho ho! One is one and all alone and ever more shall be so!

MAUDIE. Whooh!

KAT. You know that one?

MAUDIE. There's fire running down my wires!

KAT. That's the only song I know.

MAUDIE. Church.

KAT. You?

MAUDIE. Say what you like about Christians, they do a good bowl of soup.

KAT *laughs.*

(*Quiet.*) There was a basket of fire.

MA. Is this a piece?

MAUDIE. Want one?

MA (*to* KAT). Sssh.

KAT. Why?

MA (*quiet*). You'll like this.

MAUDIE (*quiet*). Orange lovely spitting sparks. She opens her
    mouth to sing, the sounds are like drops cool on your face,
    your neck, they even fall inside you splat! she turns up the
    bottle, sways, he licks sweat off her arm, off her cheek and
    they fold up together, so then it's just me and Frankie
    running through all the wet, all the shine, filthy wet and
    everything's spoiled now, all his everything, new Spiderman
    T-shirt, Spiderman trainers, it unwinds inside me too quick
    and oh! he crouches, that look when he huddles down and
    tears roll slowly down his sweet fat cheeks, his tears are
    bigger than pearls.

MA. That it?

KAT. What was that?

MA. A piece. She fishes them up sometimes. Netta and Frankie
    are always there.

KAT. Who?

MA. Another!

    MAUDIE *puts a twenty-pound note on the table.*

    I meant another piece.

    KAT *pours a shot for* MAUDIE.

    MAUDIE *drinks.*

MAUDIE. Yaroslavl!

    KAT *laughs.*

    (*Sings.*) Five for the symbols at your door, four for the
    Gospel-makers –

KAT/MAUDIE (*sing*). Three three, the rivals! Two two, the
    lily-white boys, clothèd all in green –

ALL (*sing*). Ho ho! One is one and all alone and evermore shall be so!

MAUDIE *slaps down another twenty-pound note*.

MA. No!

KAT *pours* MAUDIE *a shot, then one for herself.*

They drink.

MAUDIE. Nizhny Novgorod!

KAT. Vologda!

They laugh.

MAUDIE. Another piece?

MA. Go on, little bird.

MAUDIE. I'm running. I'm looking for something, dunno if I lost it or if I just got to find it, get a stitch so I get on a bus, then I'm running again, not looking any more, just running and running and when I stop everything's gone green, supersize green, it's epic! I take off my trainers and feel the field through my feet, and it's kind without even thinking about it, the worms are busy and kind and I think maybe this is it.

KAT. The thing you've lost?

MAUDIE. So I stay in the field till I'm sure it's not.

KAT. Not? How long did you stay?

MAUDIE. Dunno. Couple of days?

KAT. Off your face on something.

MAUDIE. Maybe.

KAT. Then what?

MAUDIE. Get up, go looking again.

KAT. For the thing? What was it? Maudie?

MAUDIE. Eh?

KAT. Did you find it?

MAUDIE. Maybe the nipper was it.

MA. Frankie.

KAT. How?

MAUDIE. He was so clean. Like a flower. And wanted, she
wanted him, I did. You got no one to hold onto, you get
blown down the river, sometimes that's alright, floating,
drifting, other times it takes you and you're so wet and stuck
with mud, it hauls you up, turns and takes you under.

MA. Where is he now?

MAUDIE. Dunno. Gone.

MA (*shocked*). Not dead?

MAUDIE. They took him off her and went away with him.

MA. I don't want him to be dead.

KAT. But what was it?

MAUDIE. What?

KAT. The *thing*.

MAUDIE. What thing?

KAT. The thing you were looking for! The thing you lost!

MAUDIE. How the fuck would I know?

> MAUDIE *puts a twenty-pound note on the table.*

> KAT *pours two shots.*

MA. There are plenty of other words.

> KAT *and* MAUDIE *drink.*

MAUDIE. Novosibirsk!

KAT. Smolensk!

> *They laugh.*

MA. I know! We'll each do a piece, take turns, like a game.

MAUDIE. Yeah yeah yeah!

KAT. Since when do you like games?

MA. Since. I don't know, since always.

KAT. Name one.

MAUDIE. Pass the Parcel.

KAT. You hate games.

MA. We played games.

KAT. Never.

MAUDIE. Hide and Seek.

KAT. Pointless when you can be working.

MA. You've just forgotten.

KAT. No. Don't do that.

MAUDIE. Tail on the Donkey.

KAT (*to* MA). That's too easy.

MA. Musical Chairs!

KAT. Here's a piece, then.

MAUDIE. Epic.

KAT. I bunk off school on a windy day. I've nicked a trashy book about shiny people making money and having drug-filled sex, I sneak home and bam! you're here, I don't know why, you're always at the yard but no, so you march me outside and I tear out the pages one by one and we watch them blow away. We played *that* sort of game.

MA. I don't remember that.

MAUDIE. Not blinking at the bottom of the bucket?

MA. No.

KAT. You hated games.

MA. Well, I don't now.

KAT. Why? What's different now?

MAUDIE. Here's one.

MA. Epic.

MAUDIE. We got sparklers, two each, we're drawing on the dark, hearts, arrows, silver whirls, we can't stop singing, we link arms and run, McDonald's, milkshake and two straws, the windows are all steamed up, and she writes: U R 4 Ever!

MA *chuckles*.

MA. Your face.

KAT. Now what?

MA. Because nothing like that ever happened to you.

KAT. Omniscient, are you?

MA. You'd always come straight to the yard from school. I'd see you from the office, chatting to the drivers, smoking, trying to look sophisticated. You never thought I can't stop singing. Did you?

KAT. No.

MA. I never even heard you sing. Maudie sings all day.

KAT. You're like a demented parrot, Maudie, Maudie and me, Maudie and me.

MAUDIE *laughs*.

MA. Are you jealous?

KAT. Of *her*?

MA. You are!

KAT. Here's one.

MAUDIE. Let's have it, Captain.

KAT. It's very dark.

MAUDIE. Nice start.

KAT. The car smells of leather. He tastes of Extra Strong Mints. When he comes, he stops frowning, just for a moment. When he gets out I can see by the courtesy light there's a blob of spunk on the back seat. So I wipe it up with the sleeve of my school blazer.

MAUDIE. Ooh. Mucky one.

KAT. Mmm.

MA. Disgusting.

MAUDIE. Were you a naughty little puss then?

MA. She made that up.

MAUDIE. Did you?

MA. To provoke me. But we'll draw a veil.

KAT. Ah, the veil! No matter how much muck there is, it always covers it, so nothing ever quite happened. Abracadabra!

KAT *pours herself a shot and drinks.*

MAUDIE *puts down her remaining nine pounds.*

Nine?

MAUDIE. She's all I got.

KAT. Blown your pay?

MAUDIE. It's the prices in this bar. (*Remembering.*) But there's more!

KAT. Where?

MAUDIE *taps the strongbox.*

MAUDIE. Safe in the bank of Kat. (*Whispers.*) Let her out, puss. We might all be dead tomorrow.

KAT. No out-of-hours withdrawals.

MAUDIE. Not even for a little vloddy voddy? Write it down then.

KAT. IOU?

MAUDIE. No, *I* owe *you.*

KAT *pours three shots.*

(*Sings, fast.*) Twelve for the twelve Apostles, eleven for the eleven who went to heaven –

KAT/MAUDIE (*singing, getting faster*). Ten for the ten commandments, nine for the nine bright-shiners, eight for the April rainers, seven for the seven stars in the sky, six for the six proud walkers, five for the symbols at your door, four for the Gospel-makers –

ALL (*sing, very fast*). Three three, the rivals! Two two, the lily-white boys, clothèd all in green, ho ho, one is one and all alone and evermore shall be so!

They drink.

MA. Kirov!

KAT. Kharkov!

MAUDIE. Minsk!

MAUDIE *and* KAT *laugh.*

MA. You're slipping.

KAT. What?

MA. Must be your age.

KAT. What must?

MA. You missed it.

KAT. What you on about?

MA. Look in the ledger.

KAT *stares at her, then runs to the ledger.*

Did you write it down?

KAT. What? No. I don't know. What did I miss? Tell me.

MA. Missed it, gone!

KAT. Tell me! I don't know what I'm looking for! Say!

MA *shouts with laughter.*

MA. Kat doesn't know what to write, it's the End of Days! Scribble scribble scribble and when you think no one's looking, you stroke the columns!

KAT. And that's funny, is it?

MA. Yes!

KAT. I work like a mule because you taught me to, I flog on in my dark suits to be just like Mrs Joyless Skinflint here, but she's had a stroke or something cos now she spends a pound per Extra on treats!

MA. The yard's yours.

KAT. Easy as that.

MA *nods*.

No no no. You struggled for years, we struggled, Christ! you ached for this, Jack Hodge skewered and skinned, you didn't think I could do it, I've done it, Ma, and now –

MA. Do what you want with it. I just want to be peaceful here with Maudie.

MAUDIE. Mm.

MA. She makes me happy.

MAUDIE. Do I?

KAT. Peaceful?

MAUDIE. Do you love me, Mrs G?

MA. Of course I do.

KAT *sits down abruptly*.

KAT. Years ago if I'd agreed that price you'd have taken the skin off my hands.

MA. I wouldn't, Kat. Not really.

KAT. That's who you are, not some old girl who wants to be *peaceful* –

MA. We were always pretty good pals, weren't we?

Silence.

KAT *takes off her shirt. She has scarred skin on one flank*.

How did you get that?

KAT. Cos you don't remember?

MA. Not really.

KAT. Touch it.

MA. No.

KAT. Touch it. It might come back to you.

MA. I don't want to.

MA turns away.

I never knew you had such a thing.

KAT. At least look at it. At least give me that.

MA won't look.

MAUDIE comes close to KAT.

MAUDIE. A burn. What from?

KAT. An iron.

MAUDIE. I got one here. (*Glances over her left shoulder.*) Not
so bad as that.

KAT. I thought it meant something. Maybe it's just a weird
patch on my side.

MAUDIE. Just something that happened.

KAT. Ugly, isn't it?

MAUDIE. Yeah.

MAUDIE touches the scar gently.

*She picks up KAT's shirt, puts it on her and buttons it up,
looking at her.*

KAT pours two shots.

They drink.

KAT. Semfiropol!

MAUDIE kisses KAT on the mouth.

KAT takes MAUDIE's head gently between her hands.

KAT throws MAUDIE across the room.

KAT sits.

Silence.

MA. Maudie?

MAUDIE. Mm.

MA. I want my bed.

    MAUDIE *stumbles to her feet, rubbing her neck.*

    MAUDIE *wheels* MA *to the bed.*

    She takes MA*'s hands and pulls her up.*

    MA *holds onto her hands.*

    I'm sorry.

MAUDIE. What for?

    MA *sobs without tears, without looking at* KAT.

MA. Say it's alright.

MAUDIE. What is?

MA. Please. Say it's alright.

    KAT *bows her head.*

MAUDIE. But it isn't.

    MAUDIE *helps* MA *into bed.*

MA. My head's terrible.

MAUDIE. Close your eyes. I'll be there in a minute.

    KAT *falls asleep.*

MA. Maudie.

MAUDIE (*stroking her hair*). Sssh.

MA. My little bird.

    MA *closes her eyes.*

    MAUDIE *finishes the bit of vodka in the bottle, considering* KAT.

    MAUDIE *goes.*

    (*Slurred and slow.*) Head's awful. Can't. Somethin's. Me?

    MAUDIE *comes with the well-bucket and its rope.*

    She ties KAT *into the chair by her arms.*

    KAT *half-wakes, sleeps again.*

MAUDIE *ties* KAT*'s legs to the chair.*

MAUDIE. This bus will wait here for a change of drivers.

She puts the bucket over KAT*'s head.*

MA. Maw.

MAUDIE. The voddy's gone, Ma. Go to sleep.

MAUDIE *gets the keys from the pocket of* KAT*'s coat.*

She unlocks the strongbox.

KAT. What?

MAUDIE. Ah.

KAT. What's?

MAUDIE. Ding dong bell, pussy's in the well.

KAT. Get me.

MAUDIE. Who put her in?

KAT. Get me out.

MAUDIE. Maudie.

KAT *shakes the bucket off her head.*

She takes in her tied state and strains against good knots, then stops.

KAT. This wasn't part of the plan.

MAUDIE *takes the notes, coins and pliers out of the strongbox.*

She sets them out on the table.

You won't, though. You don't have the balls.

MAUDIE. No balls here, Captain. Wisest thing'd be tip you down the stairs, break you to bits, then drop you in the well with old Bromwich.

KAT. But you won't.

MAUDIE. Someone needs to look after Ma.

KAT. Don't call her Ma, she's not your ma.

MAUDIE. Might as well be.

KAT. Ma!

MAUDIE. She loves me. Does she love you?

KAT. Ma!

MAUDIE. She's all in.

KAT. Ma!

MAUDIE. Just you and me, Kitty Kat. It was so simple when you were gone, we were epic. Now.

MAUDIE *brings the knife out of her apron pocket.*

KAT. What you want?

MAUDIE. I dunno yet.

KAT. Take the money and go, I should.

MAUDIE. Mm.

KAT. You can go running and looking again, you can –

MAUDIE. Ssh.

MAUDIE *holds the point of the knife just below* KAT*'s eye.*

I knew a one-eyed cat once. He managed. Had to be on guard all the time or the other cats stole his food, poor puss. Goes without saying he weren't a looker.

KAT. You wouldn't.

MAUDIE. Quick as you like and it's blinking in the bottom of the bucket.

KAT. There's a few thousand. Take it.

MAUDIE. Thanks very much, very excellent truly. Not hard to give, though, is it? Even for Miss Joyless Skinflint here. What will you give to save your eye?

KAT. What you want?

MAUDIE. Something *hard*.

MAUDIE *fishes a chicken leg out of the pot.*

Tell me about the iron.

KAT. There was a boy. He washed the cars.

MAUDIE (*eating*). How old were you?

KAT. Fifteen.

MAUDIE. Good looking, was he?

KAT *shrugs*.

Go on.

KAT. Sometimes I helped him out with jobs. I thought we were just mates, then he pulled me into the bit under the stairs and kissed me.

MAUDIE. Naughty puss.

KAT. Don't think he thought about it again. I couldn't stop. Then he stole a pair of driving gloves. I said it was me, but she found out. Better than a bloodhound. She sacked him. Then the thing with the iron.

MAUDIE. Why d'you let her do it?

KAT. Let her?

MAUDIE. Fifteen? Tall and strong, weren't you?

KAT. I deserved it.

MAUDIE. Did you?

KAT. Lying. Being soft.

MAUDIE. How she do it?

KAT. In the garage. Dad had gone to bed. We stood in the dark by his workbench, waiting for the little red light on the iron to click off.

MAUDIE. Was you scared?

KAT. Of the pain? Very.

MAUDIE. Did you say things?

KAT *shrugs*.

What did you say?

Silence.

MAUDIE *holds the knife below* KAT's *eye*.

KAT. Please. I said please don't. I said I'm sorry I'm sorry I'm sorry I'm sorry I'm sorry.

MAUDIE. And when she took no notice?

KAT. The water closed over my head.

MAUDIE. Then?

KAT. I felt sick. For days.

MAUDIE. With the pain?

KAT. And the shame.

MAUDIE *takes away the knife*.

MAUDIE. First time you give me something. Pity it's cos I got a knife in my hand.

MAUDIE *pulls the trunk from under the bed*.

See what else you got beating about in there. Cos by any reckoning you owe me big time.

KAT *strains against the ropes and rocks her chair*.

KAT. Ma!

MAUDIE. You'd call for her when she done that to you?

KAT. Help!

MA *stirs*.

Ma!

MA. Maw?

MAUDIE *goes and strokes* MA's *hair*.

KAT. Tell her to stop!

MAUDIE. Sssh.

MA. Maw.

KAT. Ma?

MAUDIE. Try to sleep now. Sssh.

MA *settles back to sleep.*

KAT *gives up.*

MAUDIE *opens the trunk and gets out a dark suit.*

She takes off her apron, KAT*'s dress and reluctantly her McDonald's cap.*

KAT. Why d'you love that scummy hat so much?

MAUDIE. Netta give it me. M for Maudie, see?

MAUDIE *puts on the suit.*

KAT. Has your entire sad fuck-up of a life been played out in McDonald's, lurching over the cold fries and slipping in ketchup?

MAUDIE. Ronald McDonald has certainly seen some golden moments.

MAUDIE *picks up the knife.*

Right then, Top Cat. A woman's got to pay her debts. What you got?

KAT *shrugs.*

MAUDIE *holds the knife blade in the candle flame.*

I already done it once, you should know that. Self-defence it was, and him heartless as a stone, can't say I planned it exactly, but I did take out his eye. Shocking how easy it is. Screwdriver. Blood and goo everywhere, him sat sobbing on the bank. Sobbing, him! As good as the loaves and fishes that was, we stood and stared. Then we legged it.

MAUDIE *tests the blade.*

Fuck, that's hot. Isn't it?

MAUDIE *touches* KAT*'s arm quickly with the knife.*

KAT *cries out.*

Oooh. Now I feel it. Isn't it lovely? Now I want to.

KAT. What you want me to say?

MAUDIE. The iron.

KAT. I told you!

MAUDIE. The water closes over your head, you're sick for days, that it?

KAT. Yes!

MAUDIE. Then what you do it to me for?

Silence.

Two roads. You could've took the other one, had a different life. What you do it to me for?

KAT. Cos it gives me a buzz. You're buzzing. I can see it in your eyes.

MAUDIE. Yeah yeah yeah. What else?

KAT. To see if you'd fight back. I wanted you to fight back.

MAUDIE. Enjoying this, then, are you? Sick with shame, you said. Say about that.

Silence.

MAUDIE *brings the knife up in front of* KAT'*s face.*

KAT *(slowly)*. Sometimes. Just as I'm waking up I see it – it's like looking down on it – a tiny me, prised open on a garage floor. It's disgusting. That's why you do it. You just want to get rid of that. So you do it and do it, cos it's the only way.

MAUDIE. It's not disgusting. It's epic.

KAT. Ugly. Pathetic.

MAUDIE. It's sad, you idiot, it's super fucking sad.

MAUDIE *puts down the knife.*

You don't understand anything, do you?

KAT *(realising)*. No.

MAUDIE *brushes her hair.*

MAUDIE. That piece you said, the mucky one in the car. Was it true?

KAT *nods*.

Who with?

KAT. A driver.

MAUDIE. Just him?

KAT. A few of them.

MAUDIE. To get even with her?

KAT *nods*.

Did you ever like it, though?

KAT. Not then.

MAUDIE. Nor me. And now?

KAT *shrugs*.

You do do it?

KAT. I have it how I want it now.

MAUDIE. How d'you manage that, Captain?

KAT. If you pay.

MAUDIE. Oh! And is there delight?

KAT. Delight?

MAUDIE. I always thought it was something people go on about and really it was just a creepy way to make you scared, but she shown me a different way and there it was.

MAUDIE *puts on her cap*.

Delight.

MAUDIE *sits on* KAT*'s lap*.

They look at each other.

An eye for an eye.

MAUDIE *kisses* KAT*'s eyelids*.

MAUDIE *gets up and counts the money*.

How d'you get to Bristol?

KAT. Going back?

MAUDIE. Dunno yet.

KAT. Paddington.

MAUDIE. That's it.

KAT. Back to Netta?

MAUDIE. There isn't Netta.

KAT. What happened?

MAUDIE. Three thousand four hundred pound. Epic. I might have a ladies' wash at the station and go first class.

MAUDIE *puts the cash in the strongbox, then* KAT*'s dress, the hairbrush and some silver cutlery from the table, which she wraps in her apron.*

KAT. You won't leave me like this?

MAUDIE. Why not?

KAT. She needs help.

MAUDIE. So I turn you loose and you have the knife off me and cut my throat?

KAT. I won't. I wouldn't. Trust me.

MAUDIE. I don't, though, Captain. That's the thing, isn't it?

MAUDIE *opens the door.*

A faint grey light comes through it.

Almost light.

MA *stirs and shivers.*

No need for that.

MAUDIE *gets onto the bed.*

She likes a good rub.

She rubs MA*'s back.*

(*Sings.*) Dem bones dem bones gonna walk around –

MA. Maw.

MAUDIE (*rubbing*). And you'll sing to her, won't you? She likes a verse. (*Sings.*) Dem bones dem bones gonna walk around –

MA. Maw.

MAUDIE. You look tuckered out, Ma. You need a long lovely lie-down.

MAUDIE *puts her arms round* MA, *rocks her and strokes her hair.*

(*Sings.*) Dem bones dem bones gonna walk around, now hear the word of the Lord!

MA *settles.*

KAT (*quiet*). What you done to her?

MAUDIE. Nothing.

KAT. She's like another person.

MAUDIE. She's just scared.

KAT. Ma?

MAUDIE. Why not?

MAUDIE *kisses* MA *on the cheek and lays her down.*

She picks up the strongbox, goes to the door, stops on the threshold.

I'd stay, you know. Can you credit it? And it hurts me that I can't. Can you credit that?

KAT. So what's the plan?

MAUDIE. No plan. See what turns up.

MAUDIE *goes.*

After a moment, MA *stirs.*

MA. Maw?

KAT. Can't help you, Ma, I'm tied up right now. Ho ho.

KAT *shuffles her chair towards the bed.*

Gradually the light coming through the door gets brighter.

Clothèd all in green, ho ho. God, you look terrible. Migraine?

MA *struggles to open her eyes and sit up a little.*

I feel like a bomb went off and blew off my clothes. I thought she'd do it. She wanted to.

MA. Maw.

KAT. An eye for an eye and she sits in my lap like an apple. I mean, two of her teeth I took! And all the rest of it. And she kisses me, plump! And for a split second – there was delight.

MA. Maw!

KAT (*realising what* MA *means*). She's gone.

MA *cries out, desolate.*

MA *stretches out her hand to* KAT, *who looks at it.*

I can't imagine you and me at breakfast tomorrow. Can you? Try. You trying?

MA. Maw.

KAT. And what if we did open? What would be *in* us? Fear that scorches the walls? Tears that flood the street? Maybe nothing. Or maybe little horns. Tender. Waving.

MA *touches* KAT*'s hair.*

I don't know how to live.

The sun rises.

KAT *watches the sunrise through the door.*

End.